KISS
'76
TWELVE MONTHS THAT DEFINED THE HOTTEST BAND IN THE LAND
Martin Popoff

Paul Stanley, Peter Criss, Ace Frehley, and Gene Simmons, in Amsterdam, May 23. The band's first European campaign was one of many milestone events for Kiss in 1976.

CONTENTS

PROLOGUE

Kiss just seem like the perfect band for birthdays, and in that spirit, myself, my editor Dennis Pernu, and the rest of the team at good ship Motorbooks back in 2024 released a little something called *Kiss at 50*. The enthusiastic response to that book got us thinking about upcoming anniversaries related to Paul Stanley, Gene Simmons, Ace Frehley, and Peter Criss, and immediately the American Bicentennial year, which saw the release of not one but two absolutely iconic Kiss albums, came to mind.

From there came the quick realization that 1976 was the most magical year in Kiss history, as the band bound into January on big boots, promoting one of the greatest live albums of all time. They then popped out two of their most cherished studio albums, both within the same year. *Destroyer* arrived in March and *Rock and Roll Over* in November, with the first of those also kicking off globally the band's first-rate Kiss Army fan club, providing for us a community and literally a badge of honor with which to defend our obsessive fandom.

So, the premise for the book became a celebration of the band's activities throughout the entire year, but with a twist. I've always been interested in this idea of the media bubble, or bubbles in general, when it comes to being a rock 'n' roll fan, sometimes curiously winding up with a situation where a fan might be into one band exaggeratedly way above any other or even declare that they are a fan of only one band.

In fact, for some reason, I remember Dave Mustaine from Megadeth saying once, weirdly, that Megadeth fans only like Megadeth. I'm sure it was just an offhand, never-repeated thing, or possibly even a misquote, but that always stuck with me as bizarre. It might have been during a time when Mustaine was most competitive with Metallica, and he perhaps meant that fans pick either one or the other. That seems more sensible to point out and more sensible to be true. There was definitely some of that when it came to the Beatles and the Rolling Stones, and I recall similar debates pitting fans of Led Zeppelin against those of Black Sabbath.

In 1976, it seemed like it went two ways: You could like all the heavy bands as well as Kiss, or it was Kiss against everybody, most notably Blue Öyster Cult and Aerosmith and, for a brief spell in 1974, the New York Dolls.

That is one of the rivulets of this book, one sort of bubble discussion, among others. In fact, the entirety of *Kiss '76* can be seen as a study of what Kiss were up to month to month, along with how important their movements and moments were in relation to whatever else was going on in 1976. This includes what was going on with the band's competition, whether other heavy rock bands or other rock and pop acts in general. Casting the net wider, we look at the band's competition for entertainment dollars outside of the music industry, in the realms of TV and movies and even sports. And then there's the outer layer of the onion, concerning what was happening in the real world completely outside of entertainment, most centrally in the realm of politics.

In other words, *Kiss '76* becomes a celebration not only of Kiss across twelve months but also of the year 1976 in general. In that respect, it's a book about Kiss not at all in a bubble, of Kiss operating in the world in which not everybody is Kiss-obsessed. Again, what's always interested me—and yet I've never really explored it in a book—is this idea of a corrective maneuver that says, Look, there's more to life beyond this band you are writing about. Heck, there are rock 'n' roll stories that were happening during that very month that were several multiples more important than what you seem to be intimating was the marquee event of that month or that year (or that decade). And then, believe it or not, there was a whole life-and-death world outside of rock 'n' roll.

And therein lies the challenge that resulted in the book you now hold in your hands. Let's talk about 1976 but from the point of view of a krazy Kiss fan who was there. In other words, this is the story of 1976 by someone with way too much Kiss on the brain. That was pretty much me, being thirteen at the time and already three or four years into being a massive rock fan but also inquisitive about the outside world—I can't prove it to you because it's long gone, but I'd made a huge scrapbook of Nixon/McGovern in 1972 . . . and I'm from Canada and was *nine*. Point is, this book made for a pretty cool idea, with the process being a sort of curative to myself that there was more to life in 1976 than getting the angles of the S's right on the Kiss logos all over my schoolbooks.

In that light, I hope you enjoy this re-creation of 1976—and the role Kiss have in it. I imagine that for many of you, as for myself, the book will conjure into a full-on reminiscence of that hallowed Bicentennial year. In other words, fingers crossed that the following pages bring back a ton of great memories beyond what the heroes of our story accomplished during that legend-making twelve-month period.

New York City, June 24. Fresh from their first European tour, the band takes care of some publicity duties (including this test walk of their new costumes) before beginning the tour cycle proper in support of *Destroyer*.

Alternate shot from the cover shoot for the self-titled debut, issued February 18, 1974. The album only got to #87 on the *Billboard* charts, despite a healthy bit of press on both sides of the Atlantic.

INTRODUCTION

A gallery of glam, all of it from the UK but one—namely, the New York Dolls, who were direct competitors to Kiss pre-'76. Represented twice, Slade are a stated direct influence on the band, particularly Paul and Gene.

The road to Kiss's triumphant 1976 was not particularly long—pretty much exactly three years—but that doesn't mean a lot of sweat and tears and desperation weren't squeezed into that action-packed timeframe. To be sure, there was some pre-Kiss dues-paying, with Wicked Lester and Chelsea and other more casual weekend bands, but the can-do team of Paul Stanley and Gene Simmons, along with the wobblier Peter Criss and Ace Frehley, had themselves an accomplished album—and more importantly, a shocking and impressive visual presentation—by February 1974, a little more than a year after Ace made the classic lineup complete in December 1972.

In context (and in the spirit of this book), Kiss were injecting themselves into the conversation as somewhat of a glam band just as the glam rock era was winding down in the United Kingdom. That movement was fronted by the likes of David Bowie, David Essex, T. Rex, Suzi Quatro, Mott the Hoople, Mud, Sweet, and Slade, and indeed at the outset, Kiss, particularly Paul, had tried on some baubles that connected them to that scene. More pertinently, the sound of the *Kiss* album, issued February 18, 1974, reflected what Slade and Sweet were doing, namely supporting the "knees-up" heavy rock end of a genre that frankly delivered some pretty embarrassing music, not to mention horrible fashion choices. In particular, Slade must be stressed, because they are an admitted and repeatedly cited influence. But there really wasn't a glam scene in the United States, and *Kiss* didn't set the world on fire. Despite three singles—"Nothin' to Lose" upon the release of the album, "Kissin' Time" in May, and "Strutter" in August—the album only got to #87 on the *Billboard* charts, notwithstanding a healthy bit of press on both sides of the Atlantic.

As alluded to, glam didn't exactly "take" in America, but Alice Cooper kind of fit, with Kiss drawing somewhat from that band's hard-hitting Detroit rock sound as well as Cooper's distinct and creepy makeup around the eyes. Locally, in the band's hometown of New York City, there was Lou Reed, moved on from the Velvet Underground, plus a band Kiss was compared to a lot: the New York Dolls. Also local but less glam was Aerosmith, who were

The trilogy of records from which *Alive*! came alive.

splitting time between Boston and New York due to the band's management company, Leber Krebs, being based in the city. Another direct comparative was Blue Öyster Cult, who split their time between Long Island and downtown. The connective tissue between BÖC and the Dictators was manager Sandy Pearlman, with the Dictators in turn being connected to the Ramones and Television and CBGB due to the band's arguably crossover punk/heavy metal sound.

Kiss followed up the debut with *Hotter Than Hell* on October 22, 1974, and *Dressed to Kill* on March 19, 1975. Suddenly, this was a serious band, recording for a shiny new label called Casablanca and getting their fair share of record reviews, interviews, and live notices that were not translating into album sales. The first tour took place immediately after the issue of the debut album, so they were busy being an international act as well, with their first show outside of New York State being in Edmonton, Alberta!

Only one single, "Let Me Go, Rock 'n' Roll," was issued in support of *Hotter Than Hell*, with the album faring even worse than the debut, stalling at #100 on *Billboard*. *Dressed to Kill* reached a promising #32, promoted by two singles, "Rock and Roll All Nite" at the time of release and "C'mon and Love Me," issued July 10, 1975.

To widen our context, after three albums, Kiss operated in a hard rock environment competing power chord for power chord with the likes of Bachman-Turner Overdrive, Queen, Rush, Thin Lizzy, and ZZ Top. By April 1975, Aerosmith had surpassed Kiss with a couple of hits in "Dream On" (which got even bigger upon rerelease in 1976) and "Walk This Way" and "Sweet Emotion," both from the new *Toys in the Attic* album. The New York Dolls were gone after two fine but misunderstood records, but Blue Öyster Cult were in ascendance with three studio albums and a double live album, establishing a pattern soon to be followed by their crosstown rivals. Queen was also on the march, with the band's fourth album, *A Night at the Opera*, doing well due to the inclusion of a little something called "Bohemian Rhapsody."

Higher up the food chain you had Black Sabbath, Deep Purple, Led Zeppelin, the Who, and the Rolling Stones. There really was very little on that scale from an American standpoint, other than maybe Alice Cooper, now gone solo. On January 8, 1975, Led Zeppelin sold out three shows at Madison Square Garden in a matter of hours. This was a couple days after a riot took place in Boston, as Led Zeppelin fans waited in the lobby of the Boston Garden to buy tickets to see the world's biggest hard rock band. Meanwhile, the Rolling Stones were mounting their famous *Tour of the Americas '75*, playing a combination of arenas and stadiums in the summer of '75, and the Who issued *The Who by Numbers* and set a record for the largest indoor concert ever, playing Michigan's Pontiac Silverdome on December 6, 1975, in front of seventy-eight thousand fans. Three weeks later, Elvis Presley played his biggest show ever, at the same venue. Closer to Kiss in temperament, Alice Cooper spent 1975 mounting the elaborate *Welcome to My Nightmare* tour, rivaling Kiss in terms of risky and expensive theatrics.

At the lighter end, Elton John, the Eagles, Linda Ronstadt, Wings, and Chicago were big deals, and prog rock was still going strong with the likes of Yes, ELP, Genesis, and Jethro Tull. Most notably, on September 12, 1975, Pink Floyd followed up their breakthrough *The Dark*

Tunnel vision. Gene, Paul, Peter, and Ace in 1975, inching closer to our landmark year.

"Get the firehouse!" Kiss take over Cadillac, Michigan, October 9, 1975.

Side of the Moon album with *Wish You Were Here*. Disco was cranking up as well (built on the foundation of a strong market for soul and R&B), with the Bee Gees getting themselves a platinum-selling single with "Jive Talkin'." In October, Bruce Springsteen appeared on the covers of both *Newsweek* and *Time*.

All of this was happening in a world where the Vietnam War was still going on, although about to wind up (badly) in April 1975. President Gerald Ford, having succeeded Richard Nixon after the latter's resignation due to the Watergate scandal, endured a couple of assassination attempts in September 1975.

On a lighter note, the Pittsburgh Steelers, the Cincinnati Reds, the Philadelphia Flyers, and the Golden State Warriors all won their respective championships; *Saturday Night Live* debuted (as *NBC's Saturday Night*); and a US/Soviet linkup in space warmed the Cold War somewhat. But the United States had also just gone through an oil crisis, which had dampened economic output, not to mention caused a vinyl shortage. (Alice Cooper and Black Sabbath band members have told the author about not being able to print enough copies of *Billion Dollar Babies* and *Sabbath Bloody Sabbath*, respectively, due to Warner Bros. having to compete for scant resources.)

But back to Kiss, beyond the headline-grabbing stories about the band's smoke and fire and face paint, it's interesting to ponder what kind of music they were making. I've often described the songs across the first three records as a cross between BTO and Slade, with a little bit of Cactus and Mountain chucked in. In other words, it was simple and traditional but heavy, quite chordal. It certainly didn't sound like British heavy metal, with its classical and/or "doom" leanings. Nor was it as finicky as Aerosmith from *Get Your Wings* forward or Ted Nugent as a solo act or even Montrose, who were three records deep by 1975. Another way of putting it: Kiss sounded like the old heavy stand-alone Sweet singles written by Mike Chapman and Nicky Chinn, as opposed to the brainier stuff on *Sweet Fanny Adams* and *Give Us a Wink*. Kiss sounded like Rush before Neil Peart joined (and definitely not after, even if that's when the two bands would meet and become chums).

The magic of those early Kiss songs as examples of tight, connectable Beatle-esque song construction would be confirmed when on September 10, 1975, Casablanca issued the two-LP *Alive!* album. Suddenly it was apparent that the band was writing in an intentioned manner, knowing that songs with big beats and lots of space and stacked power chords would come "alive" when performed live, accompanied by throngs of fans in the background howling for more.

With the *Alive!* album dominating, Paul, Gene, Ace, and Peter made plans for what would be a momentous 1976, logging their first recording sessions toward a fourth studio album September 3–6, 1975, at Electric Lady, following rehearsal sessions in August at Magna Graphic Studios, which, besides being small, limited the band to four-track demo recording. And with *Alive!* fresh in the shops—fat with additional paper goodies and gatefold—manager Bill Aucoin fired up what would become one of the great PR machines in rock history by commandeering his charges in a takeover of Cadillac, Michigan, complete with a helicopter, a mayoral welcome, a parade, and lots of high school football (which wouldn't be complete without cheerleaders).

A month later, November 21 saw the informal origins of the Kiss Army, and then a month after that, December 4, the band celebrated the *Alive!* album receiving its Recording Industry Association of America (RIAA) gold certification. Kiss closed out 1975 with a landmark New Year's Eve show at Nassau Coliseum on Long Island, playing to thirteen thousand fans. Tables turned, and Blue Öyster Cult were direct support, with an earlier chapter of American hard rock history being represented by the Leslie West Band opening the festivities. But yes, exactly a year previous on New Year's Eve, the Cultsters were headlining and Kiss supporting, and in a venue with a 3,400 capacity. For this night's festivities, however, all the band members' parents were invited to a show for the first time, and because of a mishandling of the ticket situation, friends and family watched the bands from seating assembled onstage. The special guests were delivered in stretch limos, and following the show, there was a pool party on the top floor of the Excelsior Hotel.

All of this had happened in almost exactly three years, putting Kiss on a unique path to success that would reach its fruition the following year. I'm calling it "unique" because, put in perspective, in 1975, the organization, which included Aucoin and Neil Bogart back at the office, would not rake in record sales and healthy net live receipts like most other big bands of the era, instead just barely getting by with a large supply of smoke and mirrors.

In other words, with much credit to Aucoin and the fast-and-loose business environment at Casablanca, at the tail end of 1975 it appeared that Kiss alit from some distant planet and became the biggest band in the world, when nothing could be further from the truth. "You wanted the best and you got it—the hottest band in the land, Kiss!" That's the fuse that lights up *Alive!*, and that's what all of us angry young metalheads believed. Now it was time to make the rest of the world believe it.

Kiss receives their *Alive!* gold records backstage at the Nassau Coliseum, Long Island, New York, December 31, 1975. *Alive!* had certified gold on December 4, allowing the band to usher in 1976 with a bang.

JANUARY

FEBRUARY
MARCH
APRIL
MAY
JUNE
JULY
AUGUST
SEPTEMBER
OCTOBER
NOVEMBER
DECEMBER

Kiss '76: Ace and Peter ponder their places in the band while Paul and Gene make moves to assert that they *are* the band.

JANUARY '76 TOUR DATES

January 23	**County Fieldhouse**	**Erie, PA**
January 25	**Cobo Hall**	**Detroit, MI**
January 26	**Cobo Hall**	**Detroit, MI**
January 27	**Cobo Hall**	**Detroit, MI**
January 30	**Rose Arena**	**Mount Pleasant, MI**
January 31	**Hara Arena**	**Dayton, OH**

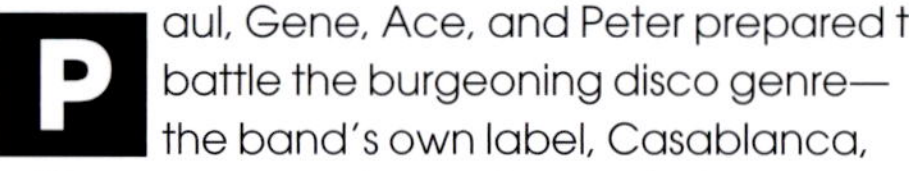

Paul, Gene, Ace, and Peter prepared to battle the burgeoning disco genre—the band's own label, Casablanca, will become a major participant in the controversial dance music format—with what would become their fourth studio album, working at the Record Plant in New York beginning January 4. Producer Bob Ezrin had signed on after meeting the band in Toronto and in New York City and then (about a year later, according to Ezrin) taking in a live performance in Saginaw, Michigan, August 15, 1975.

Given the importance of the band's visual presentation in pictures and onstage, they were working on new costumes, which were debuted through a publicity shoot at A&R Studios on January 13. Typical of Kiss kaos, Ace's and Peter's boots weren't ready yet, so they wore the old ones. Also, they wouldn't use the new outfits right away, sticking with the iconic *Alive!* look until the first date of the *Spirit of '76* tour in Norfolk, Virginia, on July 6. The *Alive!* stage wear would make their last appearance when the band showed up at the Borden Chemical Company on May 25, 1977, to add their blood to the ink used to print their first Marvel Comic.

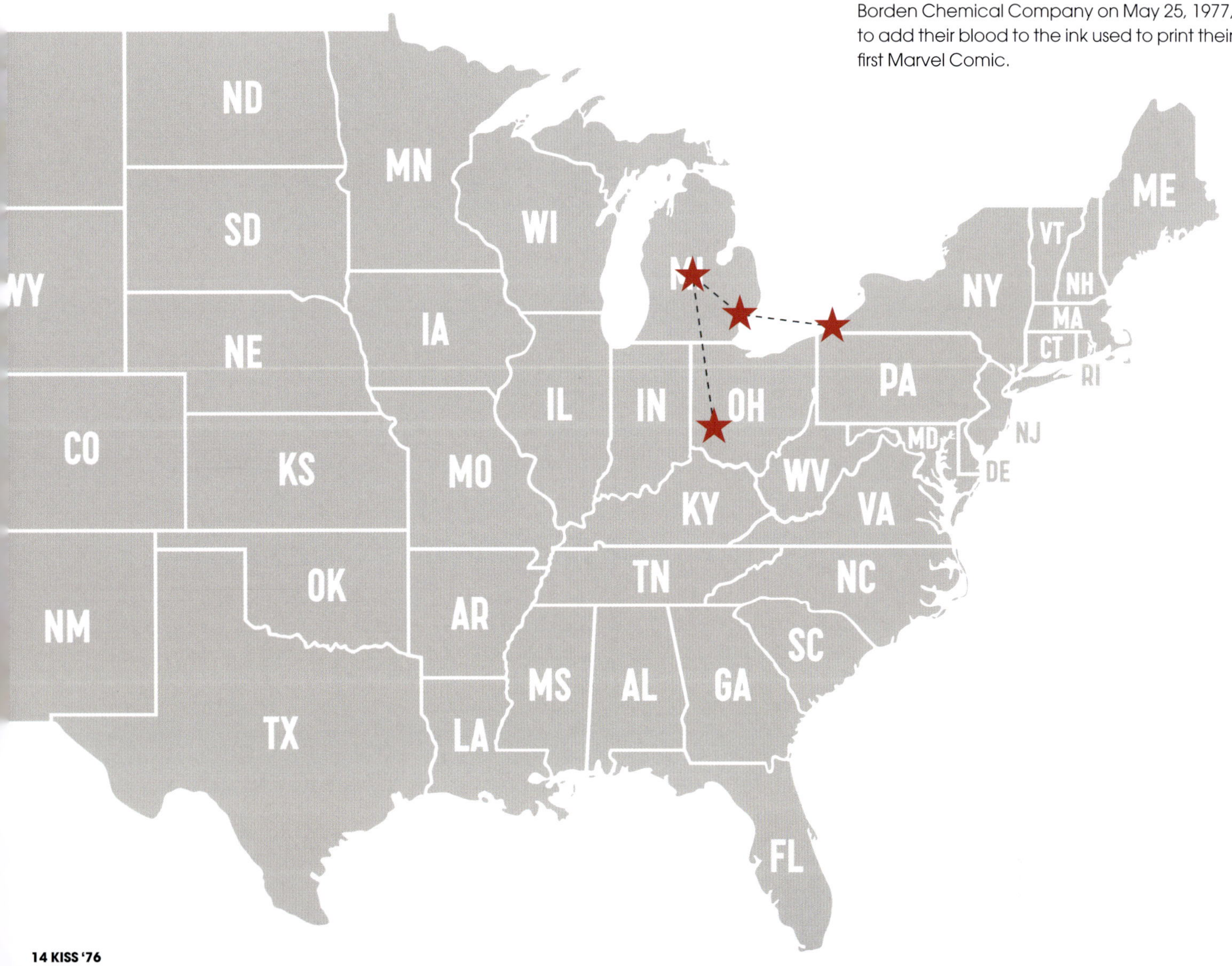

Partying it up with *Deep Throat* porn star Linda Lovelace and concert promoter Ron Delsener backstage after the band's New Year's Eve show at Nassau Coliseum, December 31, 1975.

Also on January 13, the band was present in full regalia to witness the choral arrangements and orchestral bits recorded for "Great Expectations" and "Beth." Everybody in the orchestra was given tuxedo shirts for the occasion, while the production crew wore white gloves. The singing was done by the Brooklyn Boys Choir.

On January 20, Paul celebrated his twenty-fourth birthday, and two days later the band was preparing for upcoming tour dates by conducting rehearsals at Carroll Musical Instrument Rentals in New York City. The next night they played a warm-up gig at the County Field House, in Erie, Pennsylvania. Opening was local prog rock act Phillippe, called into action when Lou Gramm's pre-Foreigner band Black Sheep were no-shows.

The January 20 edition of *Circus* magazine ran a four-page feature on the *Alive!* album, which was advertised on the back cover. (The front cover featured Ray and Dave Davies from the Kinks.) Other acts getting prominent features in the issue were George Harrison, Jethro Tull, and Aerosmith. The *Circus* Top 20 spotted Kiss's *Alive!* at #2, while Black Sabbath's *Sabotage* took #1 and Aerosmith's *Toys in the Attic* was #3. Kiss's dominance of the chart was seen with *Dressed to Kill* showing up at #6 and *Hotter Than Hell* at #13. However, the *Circus* Magazine/Shure Modern Music Makers Awards 1975, published in this issue and generated from thousands of votes from *Circus* readers, were entirely Kiss-free. "Best Group" was awarded to Led Zeppelin, followed by the Rolling Stones and the Who.

On January 24, Kiss hold a formal press concert at the Detroit Metropolitan Wayne County Airport (DTW) in advance of three sold-out dates at Cobo Hall. They had flown from New York in style, renting a Learjet. Also on this day, the live version of "Rock and Roll All Nite" peaked at #12 on *Billboard*, after eleven weeks on the grid (with four to come). With respect to the wider hit album from the previous year having risen to #9 on the *Billboard* grid at the tail end of 1975, *Alive!* reached #9 again on this day, maintaining that position for three weeks.

IN WORLD NEWS...

The boldest year in Kiss history coincided with American Bicentennial festivities as the country celebrated two hundred years since independence from Great Britain. The party kicks off on the first day of the year, when the Liberty Bell in Philadelphia is moved from Independence Hall to a newly erected facility more fitting of the occasion.

On January 10, the world loses bluesman Howlin' Wolf to congestive heart failure at the age of sixty-five, and two days later, foremost mystery writer Agatha Christie dies at the age of eighty-five.

In pop culture outside of music, *Mary Hartman, Mary Hartman*, a situation comedy that spoofs soap operas, debuts, lasting just

"You've got great expectations!" Kiss with the Brooklyn Boys Choir at A&R Studios on January 13.

January 25, 26, and 27 comprised the Cobo Hall stand. The first performance at the 12,600-capacity arena had Back Street Crawler opening, with Rory Gallagher doing the honors on the second and third nights. The band closed out the month with a January 30 show at the Rose Arena, Mount Pleasant, Michigan (sold out, 6,000, opened by locals Hot Lucy), and a January 31 show at the Hara Arena in Dayton, Ohio (sold out, 8,000, opened by the Leslie West Band). As for the setlists, they were essentially a selection of songs reflective of the *Alive!* album, with no previews from *Destroyer* on offer.

Cobo Hall also saw the next stage in development of the Kiss Army fan club, moving on from what superfan Bill Starkey had created. Yellow flyers were distributed announcing the club, and there was an ad in the "Kiss on Tour—1976" tour program, which debuted at the first Cobo Hall show. For $5 per year, you received a set of photos, a poster, and a shirt with an iron-on design, along with quarterly newsletters.

An amusing review of the Dayton show in the *Journal Herald* read: "Yes, Kiss, the ultimate in heavy, pervo, rock groups, played to an adoring mob of boppers, freaks, straights, and even some oldsters (over 30?) and presented one of the most ridiculous, fast-paced, electrifying and hysterical shows ever to hit town. In Kiss one finds the worst aspects of every '70s super-mean rock act: volume bordering on the vomit level, absurd and tasteless costumes and makeup, childish lyrics that deal largely with death and sex, asinine

two seasons, into July 1977. *The Bionic Woman* TV show first airs on January 14, making Lindsay Wagner a pinup star for young Kiss fans. It's a spin-off of the wildly successful *The Six Million Dollar Man* featuring Lee Majors, which hit the airwaves hard in 1974. Two days later, the *Donny & Marie* show debuts, a spin-off from the multimedia Osmonds empire, followed two weeks later by *Laverne & Shirley*, a spin-off of *Happy Days*.

On January 21, the Concorde supersonic airliner launches commercial service with two simultaneous flights. Expensive and impractical, the plane will feature in anecdotes from various rock

H. A. MacMillan and members of the New York Philharmonic help "Great Expectations" and "Beth" sound lush on January 13.

stage antics, and way too many visual stunts. But I love 'em! I am so tired of intensely serious rock-and-rollers who are 'into their music' and unbelievably hip and cool that they come across as a bunch of snobs or—worse yet—musical zombies. Enter Kiss like a breath of fresh air."

Despite a growing army of fans, especially in the Detroit area, the gatekeepers at *Rolling Stone* remained firmly skeptical, with Alan Neister writing in his January 1 review of the previous year's *Alive!* album: "Kiss onstage could possibly be mildly entertaining for about ten minutes, but on record, minus the impact of gaudy painted faces and stage theatrics, the band must be judged solely for its music. It's awful. Criminally repetitive, thuddingly monotonous. And like the legions of equally talentless bands across the country, Kiss attempts to get by on volume and tired riffing. Unlike these other bands, however, they came up with the idea of dragging rock further into the pits of theatrical overkill, managing, in the process, to pick up a legion of young fans who hadn't heard these riffs in their previous incarnations (Grand Funk comes to mind). That Casablanca has decided to promote the band as new bad-boy teen idols is obvious from the packaging, a glossy, full-color, multipage insert showing all the Kisses in close-up and a suitably trippy letter from each."

stars over the years but sees limited success and is canceled in 2003.

Finally, on January 30, future US President George H.W. Bush becomes director of the CIA.

The January 20 edition of *Circus* magazine ran a four-page feature on the *Alive!* album, which was advertised on the back cover.

Creem lensman Robert Alford was on hand to capture the band arriving at Detroit Metropolitan Airport on January 24, for three nights at Cobo Hall.

IN MUSIC NEWS . . .

The month kicks off with an unfortunate incident on January 5 in which drugged-up and suicidal ex-Beatles manager Mal Evans is shot dead in a showdown with police. The following day, Peter Frampton issues *Frampton Comes Alive!*, which goes on to be the record on everybody's lips throughout the balance of the year—or at least until

Boston's debut in the summer. Their album *Boston* will reach platinum on April 8, 1976, and eventually certify eight-times platinum.

Still very much thriving, Jethro Tull issue *M.U.—The Best of Jethro Tull* on January 9, which goes gold the following month and platinum in 1978. With Kiss's *Alive!* album already certifying gold on September 1 of the previous year, Casablanca sees further success when Donna Summer's *Love to Love You Baby* goes gold on January 19. Other important records this month come from David Bowie, who issues *Station to Station* on January 23, and Bad Company, who issue *Run with the Pack* on January 30. Bowie's record goes gold almost immediately, with the Bad Company album registering platinum at the end of the year.

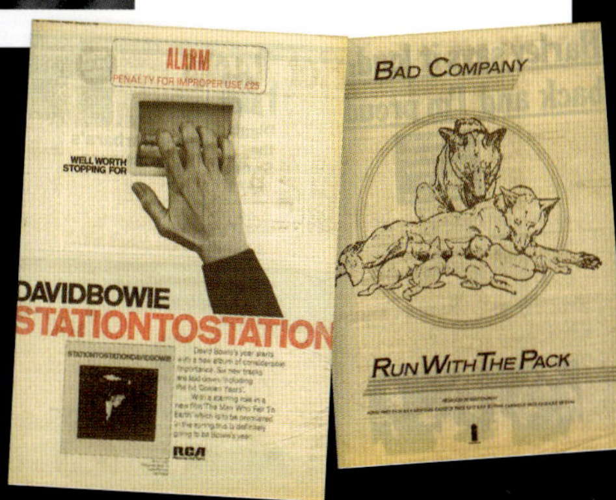

FEBRUARY

The *Alive!* costumes were soon to be replaced as the band ascended further toward superhero status.

FEBRUARY '76 TOUR DATES

February 1	**Richfield Coliseum**	**Cleveland, OH**
February 4	**Milwaukee Auditorium**	**Milwaukee, WI**
February 5	**Dane County Coliseum**	**Madison, WI**
February 6	**Civic Center (two shows)**	**St. Paul, MN**
February 9	**UT Terrace Ballroom**	**Salt Lake City, UT**
February 11	**Memorial Coliseum**	**Portland, OR**
February 12	**Spokane Coliseum**	**Spokane, WA**
February 13	**Paramount Theatre**	**Seattle, WA**
February 14	**Paramount Theatre**	**Seattle, WA**
February 16	**Adams Fieldhouse**	**Missoula, MT**
February 23	**The Forum**	**Inglewood, CA**
February 24	**The Forum**	**Inglewood, CA**
February 26	**Swing Auditorium**	**San Bernardino, CA**
February 27	**Sports Arena**	**San Diego, CA**
February 29	**Blaisdell Arena**	**Honolulu, HI**

The mix of the forthcoming *Destroyer* album was wrapped up on February 3, with the soundtrack-like intro sequence to "Detroit Rock City" completed the following day and the mastering of the album the day after that. On February 20, Kiss was added to the Hollywood Walk of Fame in front of Grauman's Chinese Theatre.

The February issue of *Hit Parader* included a short piece about the recording of the new album. "'By next year they should be the biggest group in the country,' (producer Bob) Ezrin told us. 'All they need is a hit single, and I'm going to get that out of them,' said the man who did the same for Alice Cooper."

Other than that, the band let off some steam and played some shows, beginning on February 1 at Richfield Coliseum in Cleveland with southern hard rockers Hydra supporting. Curiously, it was another heavy southern band, Point Blank, supporting at the next clutch of shows, beginning in Milwaukee, Wisconsin, on February 4. Next came Madison, Wisconsin, again on February 5; two reduced theater shows in St. Paul, Minnesota, on the same day on February 6; Salt Lake City, Utah, on February 9; Portland, Oregon, on February 11; and

(Continued on page 27)

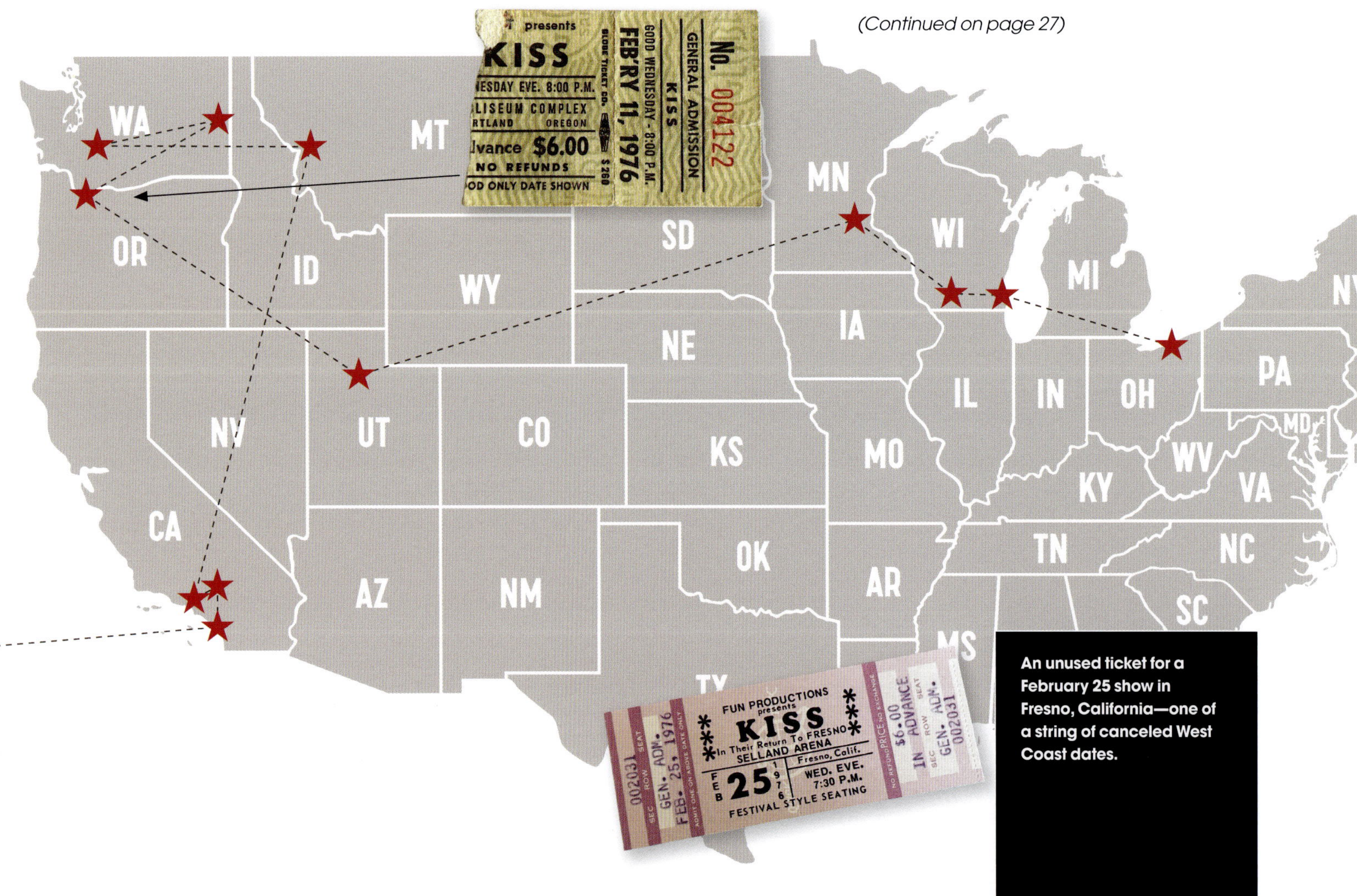

An unused ticket for a February 25 show in Fresno, California—one of a string of canceled West Coast dates.

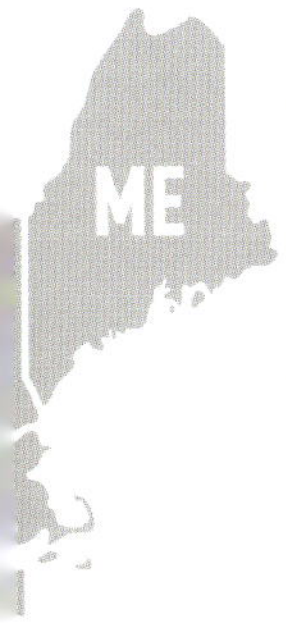

Space Ace in space boots, February 1 at Richfield Coliseum, Cleveland, Ohio.

IN WORLD NEWS...

It's more true these days, but music has always had to compete with a lot of other entertainment options. If you were in Kiss's prime demographic in 1975 and 1976—the younger end of teen males—you were likely a big *Star Trek* and *Planet of the Apes* fan, not to mention settling in after school and watching *Get Smart, Hogan's Heroes,* and *Gilligan's Island* reruns. In fact, *Star Trek* was long over by 1976 and in relentless rerun, while the last of the five original *Planet of the Apes* movies was released in 1973. Still airing in prime time was *M*A*S*H,* which kicked off in 1972 and lasted until 1983.

For those young teen Kiss fans, dreaming about driving one day

This page and following: **In February, Kiss was supported in Cleveland by hard-hitting southern rockers Hydra, who kicked off the show half an hour late due to icy local conditions around the arena.**

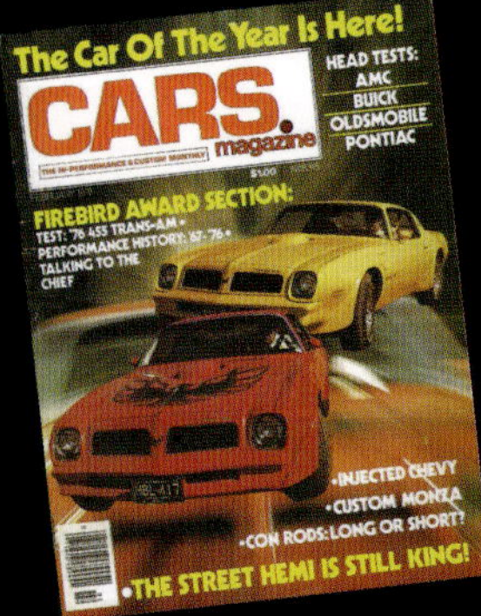

usually involved fantasies about Corvettes and Camaros, along with the new generation of Firebird, the Trans Am, introduced in 1975. If you were still playing with toys, there were LEGO, Lite-Brite, Creepy Crawlers, Hot Wheels, Matchbox, Big Jim, G.I. Joe (with kung fu grip), Major Matt Mason, Spirograph, Nerf, lawn darts, firecrackers, and a couple notable fads in mood rings and the Pet Rock. Speaking of firecrackers, they always seemed available, even in Canada, where they were banned on September 27, 1972—and they were used to blow up G.I. Joes, dolls, and model cars and airplanes.

All of these toys and activities might have been enjoyed with

a mouthful of Pop Rocks, the crackling new candy craze of 1976, although word went around that if you chased them with soda pop, your stomach would explode.

Sidestepping internal rupture and third-degree burns on the hands from strings of "lady finger" firecrackers, kids often injured themselves constructing ramp jumps for our Sting-Ray bicycles or reenacting the roller-skating violence from the 1975 movie *Rollerball*. Roller skating in general was a craze, with local "roller rinks" blaring the day's hits from a PA. The bike stuff, including careening through trails and sticking sports cards in the spokes to simulate the sound of a motor, found

Visiting the Hollywood Walk of Fame in February. Kiss wouldn't get their star until 1999, but they seemed to like Elton John's.

inspiration in the daredevil antics of Evel Knievel (basically Kiss on a motorcycle). The Evel Knievel Stunt Cycle toy (with "gyro-powered motor"), introduced in 1973, was big at the time, along with the accompanying Scramble Van. Also getting kids busted up were kung fu antics fueled by Bruce Lee movies, the *Kung Fu* TV series starring

David Carradine (though it ran out the string in 1975), and the Carl Douglas hit from 1974, "Kung Fu Fighting."

In the world of magazines, your card-carrying Kiss fan would know *Circus*, *Creem*, and *Hit Parader*, but also *Mad* and *Cracked*, arguably at their peaks in this period, and maybe *CARtoons*, which had

Inglewood, California, February '76. Note the fan art reproducing the iconic Bicentennial photo shoot.

Spokane, Washington, on February 12. Over to Seattle, the band played two sold-out dates, February 13 and 14, at the Paramount Theatre, with a capacity of three thousand. Due to a few cancellations, this leg ended February 16 at the University of Montana in Missoula.

"Talk about your dark satanic mills," wrote the *Salt Lake Tribune* in their review of the February 9 show. "Kiss could be the house band in the palace of Ming the Merciless. Kiss, which invaded the Terrace Ballroom Monday night, embodies metaphors. The one with the topknot eats fire, drips blood from his mouth and wags his snake's tongue at the audience. The lead guitarist plays a solo so hot the guitar smokes. These are not metaphors; this is what Kiss does. Call it satire; one cannot know their intentions. I liked them, and the crowd shoehorned into the ballroom screamed, waved their arms, jumped, sat on one another's shoulders, smoked grass and had a fine time: a very polite and friendly crowd, I might add."

The February 10 issue of *Circus*, with Bob Dylan on the cover, offered a short feature as part of the mag's Back Page section about the band's trip to Cadillac, Michigan, the previous month. Meanwhile, *Alive!* maintained its #2 spot in the Top 20, with *Dressed to Kill* hovering at #5, *Kiss* at #7, and *Hotter Than Hell* at #15. In other words, every Kiss album was on the popular magazine's biweekly chart. Neil Young, Patti Smith, Black Sabbath, Queen, and Earth, Wind & Fire enjoyed large features inside.

Creem put Dylan on their cover as well, while offering large features on the Who and Roxy Music.

Following a brace of canceled shows, the band performed two nights at The Forum in Inglewood, California, supported by Montrose. By this point, Ronnie had lost Sammy Hagar to a solo career, and he and new singer Bob James were supporting the band's third album, *Warner Bros. Presents Montrose!* The band was treated to a lavish after-show party and gifted free use of a Rolls-Royce Cornice while in town.

been established in 1959 but got a successful rethink in 1975. Not coincidentally, this was the height of the custom van craze as well.

In February 1976, specifically, the buzzy new movie was *Taxi Driver*, produced by Martin Scorsese and starring Robert De Niro and in theaters February 8. The gritty film noir underscored the reputation of Kiss's home turf, New York City, as a dystopian nightmare.

Speaking of nightmares, Richard Nixon was still roaming free, on February 21, visiting China with former First Lady Pat. There he met with government leaders, marking exactly four years since his historical diplomatic visit while in office. On the lighter side, the 1976 Winter Olympics vaulted figure skater Dorothy Hamill into the American consciousness, followed by her subsequent TV ads for Short & Sassy conditioner by Clairol.

Finally, at the end of the month, on February 29, the hit 1965 musical *The Sound of Music* was shown on TV for the first time, garnering a record fee of $15 million.

Following spreads: **Kiss dress-up isn't just for Halloween. A lot of fans have attended concerts as their favorite Kiss members throughout the decades.**

IN MUSIC NEWS...

On February 2, David Bowie kicks off his *Isolar—1976* (or *Isolar 1*) tour in Vancouver, British Columbia. That same day, Lynyrd Skynyrd issue their fourth album, *Gimme Back My Bullets,* which certifies gold despite having no real hits. Were Skynyrd and Kiss in competition? They certainly were framed that way in Ohio, where every Friday night on the radio they'd be pitted against each other, with older redneck fans going for Ronnie Van Zant and Co. and early teen hard rockers plumping for the flashier city guys.

Also this month, Sweet issues *Give Us a Wink,* a heavy metal classic sadly ignored outside of the minor hit "Action." Much like Thin Lizzy, Sweet released two albums

LYNYRD SKYNYRD
25
50
75
GIMME BACK MY BULLETS
GIMME BACK MY BULLETS THEIR FOURTH ALBUM HIGH ON THE CHARTS WITH LOADED BULLETS. INCLUDES THEIR SINGLE "DOUBLE TROUBLE"

that delivered the goods; much like Thin Lizzy, Sweet was derailed by substance abuse. That's two potential Kiss competitors that fell by the wayside due to drug abuse, something Gene and Paul would have to police within their own band through to the end of the decade.

February 13 represents the release date for *A Trick of the Tail,* the first Genesis album without Peter Gabriel. Progressive rock and Kiss go together like oil and water, but one thing they have in common is that the critics generally liked neither. Speaking of prog, Yes sits out 1975 and 1976 as members work on solo albums, none of which will cause much of a stir. It might be said that the new vanguard of hard rock acts in America—Kiss included—is being viewed with more excitement than those constructing prog records, much the same way punk usurped prog in the UK press.

On February 17, the Eagles issue *Their Greatest Hits (1971–1975).* It is the first album ever to be certified as platinum, which takes place on February 24. Platinum is

a new RIAA designation adopted this year for sales in excess of one million units. This follows the establishment of gold in 1958, while preceding the diamond plateau established in 1999.

The new Bob Dylan album, *Desire*, dominates the charts in February, taking the *Billboard* #1 slot for four weeks. This follows *Chicago IX: Chicago's Greatest Hits* and *Gratitude* from Earth, Wind & Fire taking the #1 position through January. The Eagles album will occupy the #1 slot on two separate occasions, but *Frampton Comes Alive!* is destined to be the biggest album of the year, taking the top spot four times.

Topping the charts song-wise for the month are "50 Ways to Leave

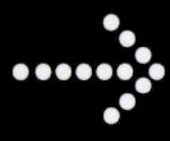

Your Lover" by Paul Simon and "Theme from S.W.A.T." by Rhythm Heritage. But many memories of this time are probably dominated by Elton John, with songs like "Philadelphia Freedom" and "Island Girl" from the previous year still in heavy rotation, along with "The Bitch Is Back" and "Bennie and the Jets" from the year before that, 1974.

Besides Elton John, other songs from the *Billboard* Top 20 tormented young Kiss fans to no end, including Barry Manilow's "I Write the Songs," Hot Chocolate's "You Sexy Thing," Neil Sedaka's "Breaking Up Is Hard to Do," Electric Light Orchestra's "Evil Woman," Nazareth's "Love Hurts," the Eagles' "Take It to the Limit," and the Who's "Squeeze Box."

Where Kiss fit into this period is interesting. The studio version of "Rock and Roll All Nite" (from *Dressed to Kill*) had topped out at #68 on the *Billboard* charts, while the rendition from *Alive!* reached #12. Soon, however, the original would replace the live version on the radio.

JANUARY
FEBRUARY
MARCH
APRIL
MAY
JUNE
JULY
AUGUST
SEPTEMBER
OCTOBER
NOVEMBER
DECEMBER

'76

Kiss kicked off March 1976 with a shiny new anthem: "Shout It Out Loud."

MARCH '76 TOUR DATES

March 4	Civic Center Music Hall	Oklahoma City, OK
March 6	Pershing Auditorium	Lincoln, NE
March 8	Assembly Center	Tulsa, OK
March 11	Von Braun Civic Center	Huntsville, AL
March 12	The Warehouse	New Orleans, LA
March 13	Exhibition Hall	Mobile, AL
March 14	Ellis Auditorium North Hall	Memphis, TN
March 20	Lakeland Civic Center	Lakeland, FL
March 21	Miami Jai-Alai Fronton	Miami, FL
March 24	Civic Center	Philadelphia, PA
March 25	War Memorial Coliseum	Johnstown, PA
March 26	State Farm Arena	Harrisburg, PA
March 27	Utica Memorial Auditorium	Utica, NY
March 28	Civic Center	Springfield, MA

The heroes of our story kicked off March 1976 with the release of their shiny new anthem "Shout It Out Loud," which also represented a completion date, of sorts, for the album to come.

And arrive it did, with *Destroyer* issued on March 15. Inside the packaging was sign-up information for the Kiss Army, which might be considered the fourth but most officious rollout of the legendary fan club. Even before the launch of *Destroyer*, the first Kiss Army kits had been sent out based on the late-January appeal, but now the quality of the communications really picked up. Eventually it got complicated, because the contents of an initial and second and third kit would vary from person to person, depending on when they joined. Generally speaking, there was a membership card, certificate, newsletter, order forms for merch, pictures and bios of the band, a discography page, posters, and patches. The initial materials were inserted in a folder emblazoned with the second-generation (and current) Kiss Army logo, designed by an associate of Dennis Woloch named Vinnie, with the band having moved on from the decal design provided by press officer Alan Miller. "Bob Steele" (in actuality, Howard Marks Agency employee Peggy Tomarkin, who would do much of the writing) was ensconced as the executive director and headquarters was established in Woodland Hills, California.

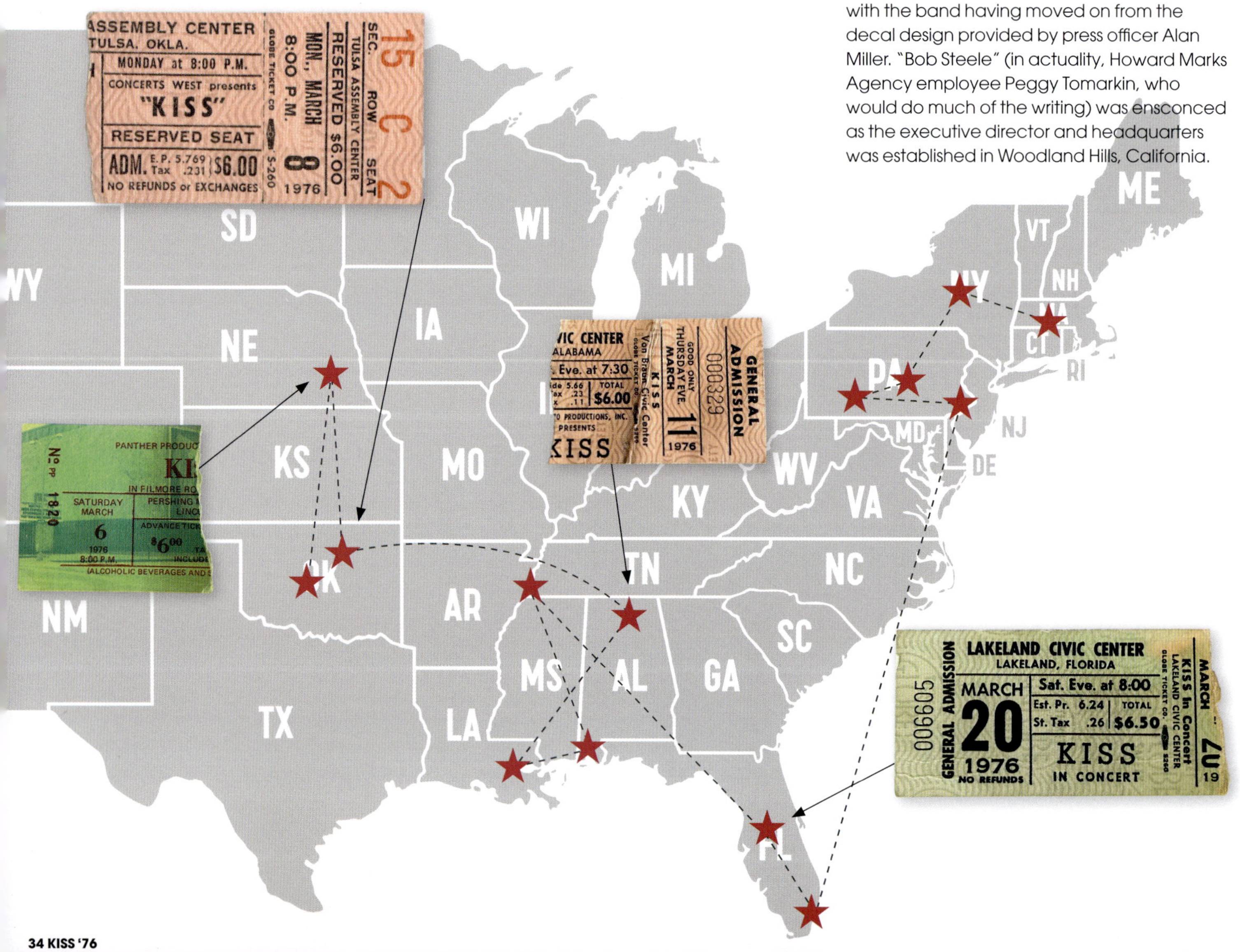

In its March 20 issue, *Billboard* reported: "Neil Bogart, president of Casablanca Records, has developed specialized market exposure targets for each artist and group on his label that is helping overcome the tight playlist problems of radio exposure. But the system requires a gamble that may run into 'hundreds of thousands of dollars' in investment before hitting the musical jackpot. "People have to see an act before they can cherish the act and make the act part of their lives," Bogart says. For this reason, Casablanca underwrote the first year of the group Kiss. "We put them out on an eighty-eight day tour through ATI. Jeff Franklin handled the tour. And we lost money on every date. But by the end of the tour, Kiss was ready to become headliners."

The "hundreds of thousands of dollars" have to be invested slowly, however, and wisely. "You can't overhype. And you have to get personally involved in the shows of an artist. If the acts will let you; some acts won't let you. Some of our acts don't want us to be involved; they want to do everything themselves. But the show is of utmost importance. As important as getting radio airplay. We proved that with Kiss. Kiss didn't get airplay, other than progressive FM airplay, until its current single 'Rock and Roll All Nite.' However, what we're talking about is an act that will go out and earn $500 to $2,500 a night and lose anywhere from $1,000 to $2,000 a night. Most groups or their managers don't have that kind of money to shell out. So, a record company has to be prepared to spend X amount of dollars."

After a few canceled shows in the South, Kiss tour duties resumed. Openers in March included Dr. Feelgood, Target, Thee Image, .38 Special, and Leber Krebs management hopefuls Artful Dodger.

"Artful Dodger was a band that was good live," David Krebs told me, "but I felt they needed to do a round of clubs. They fought me tooth and nail, saying that they were ready for arenas. I don't know if, in retrospect, this was out of some spite because they challenged me, but I got them some dates with Kiss. Obviously, they did not go over well with that audience. If they had done clubs first, then they would have been ready to play opening up for an arena band. Look, whatever rock audience you go to, you introduce a new act and it's like the Roman Colosseum. They either love you or they don't. You see the thumbs-up or the thumbs-down."

The March 25 issue of *Rolling Stone* included a feature on Kiss written by David McGee. Describing the New Year's Eve show that kicked off this momentous year for the band, McGee wrote: "Onstage were: Gene Simmons, a fire-breathing, blood-spitting bass player who stalks and lurks menacingly around stage right, fluttering rock's most lascivious tongue at swarms of young girls in front of the stage; Paul Stanley, a sensual purveyor of thunderous chords commanding center stage, prancing to and fro, masculine/feminine in whiteface with a large black star over his right eye; Ace Frehley, a self-described 'crazy kid from the Bronx; a rebel, always in trouble with the cops' making good as lead guitarist, blending speed with emotion, his lithe body floating gracefully around stage left and his mind inhabiting another plane entirely; and Peter Criss, drummer with boundless energy, high school dropout, ex-member of a Brooklyn street gang called the Phantom Lords, with black cat whiskers and silver nose."

Casablanca president Neil Bogart (center) promotes label acts, including Donna Summer (left) in 1977. Bogart's early financial support of Kiss was instrumental in their success.

In World News...

On March 1, the British House of Commons makes seatbelts mandatory. In the United States, it's done by state, with New York acting first, in 1984. Also in motoring news, two weeks later, Los Angeles institutes the first American high-occupancy vehicle (HOV) lane. The same day this happens, Kiss issue a new album with an opening song about a car crash. Down the road in Carlsbad, just north of San Diego, America gets its first-ever skateboard park amid a craze for the sport (*SkateBoarder* magazine began publishing the previous year) that broke many a Kiss fan's arm.

March 3, the same day the skate park opened, popular TV detective series *Cannon* ends its five-year

Concerning the new album, McGee wrote, "Kiss' latest album, *Destroyer*, reflects producer Bob Ezrin's vision of the band as a 'social phenomenon, a caricature of all the urges of youth.' Under Ezrin's direction, the melodies have become as strong and memorable as the riffs behind them. There's a fluency, precision and urgency now that escaped them a year ago. *Destroyer* is a radical departure from Kiss' previous albums. It works as an album of songs which convey the group's image, as, in Ezrin's words, 'symbols of just unfettered evil and sexuality,' along with taking some new directions. Criss's lyrical ballad 'Beth,' for example, proves him to be the group's best singer, and may even find its way onto some MOR playlists."

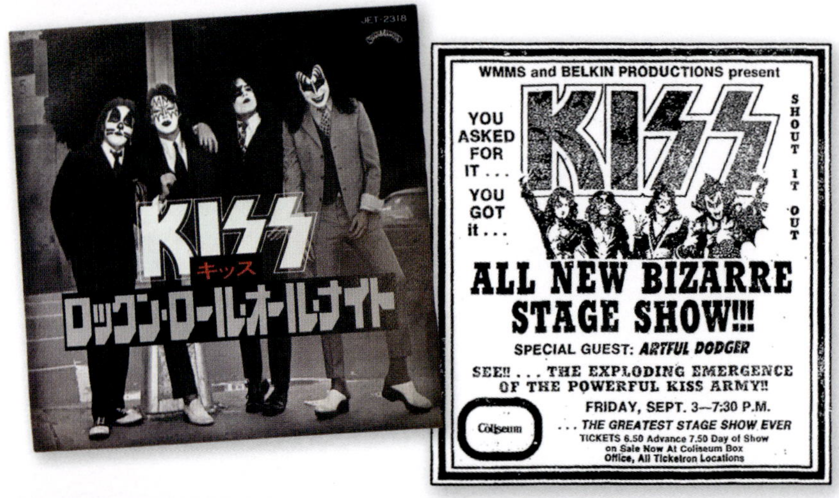

Peter, high school dropout and ex-member of a Brooklyn street gang, was about to step out from behind the kit for a vocal turn on an unlikely hit single.

run (but there's still *Kojak* and *The Rockford Files*).

Staying with heavies, on March 8, the largest observed meteor in history hits China. Weighing in at 3,894 pounds (1,766 kg), it's still the biggest observed. The event was accompanied by a meteor shower of over a hundred fragments over and expanse of 193 square-miles (500 sq km).

Staying with March 8, actor Freddie Prinze Jr. is born. At the time, his father was starring in the hit sitcom *Chico and the Man*, which aired from 1974 to 1978. (Prinze Sr. would commit suicide on January 29, 1977.) Other popular sitcoms enjoyed by young Kiss fans in the spring of 1976 include *Good Times* and *Maude* (both *All in the Family* spin-offs),

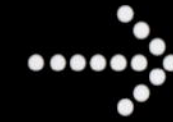

According to producer Ezrin, "Beth" proved Peter to be the band's best singer. Drum manufacturer Pearl awarded him with an endorsement deal.

"Really, what we're dealing with is emotion," added Gene, in McGee's article. "You don't always get a chance to fuck when you're horny or punch somebody in the face when you feel like it. It's frustration and it builds. Some people never let it out. They crack and they're carried away by the guys in the white coats. Our situations are 'Let your guts out!' things. You scream, and all that frustration comes out. When people become disenchanted with the world, they turn to fantasy, and here we are. We're real fantasy figures."

Later, Gene explained "We were trying to bring back flamboyance and stage show to rock 'n' roll, and we knew there'd be problems with the music. But you have to take that first step. When we started out, that's the music we were doing at that time, and that's what we were like then. I don't feel apologies are necessary, because there's simply nothing to apologize for. We've become what we are because of what we look like, obviously, and because of the music. *Destroyer* is just the second step. The music's taking the forefront."

The month ended with an update on Kiss's feisty record label, posted in *Record World* on March 27. Titled "Casablanca Reports Biggest

plus *Sanford and Son* and *Welcome Back, Kotter*, which made a star out of John Travolta, who portrayed Vinnie Barbarino, challenger to the Fonz for king of cool.

On March 16, UK Prime Minister Harold Wilson resigns, citing exhaustion (and not the rise of punk rock). On March 22, filming begins on *Star Wars*, which will become a sensation upon release in 1977, and probably present more competition for the attention of Kiss fans than anything coming out of the rock 'n' roll realm.

On March 24, Argentine President Isabel Perón is overthrown in a military coup, with the South American country making the news a second time this month

Week Ever," the piece stated, "Neil Bogart, president of Casablanca Records, Inc., has announced that the label has billed over $3 million the week of March 8–12. Said Bogart, 'This is the biggest week, and it will be the biggest month of my 13 years in the record business.' A $4 million-plus month is projected. The new Kiss LP, *Destroyer*, and Donna Summer's new album, *A Love Trilogy*, comprise most of the billing for the past week. Other LPs contributing to the current success of the label include Parliament, Angel, Buddy Miles, Hugh Masekela, Larry Santos and Margaret Singana, as well as the Kiss catalog and Donna Summer's 'Love to Love You Baby.'"

The same issue included a piece titled "Bicentennial Breakout," which reported that Ray Charles's rendition of "America the Beautiful" was being rush-released due to its popularity as background music during skating events at the Olympics, as well as on the TV special *Celebration: The American Spirit*. As we've alluded to, Kiss also contributed to the spirit of the Bicentennial year, most notably through an iconic photo shoot featuring an American flag and Peter with marching snare.

"We were trying to bring back flamboyance and stage show to rock 'n' roll," Gene later explained, "and we knew there'd be problems with the music."

after the Montoneros terrorist group detonated a bomb on March 15, coincidentally the release date for *Destroyer*. Also mid-month, violence ramps up in Northern Ireland, with four civilians killed by a bomb on March 17, followed shortly by attempted bombings in the London underground and a detonation in an above-ground garbage can on March 27. In other terrorist-related news, on March 20, Patty Hearst receives a thirty-five-year sentence for her involvement with the Symbionese Liberation Army; in the end, she serves twenty-two months. On the day of her sentencing, Linkin Park's Chester Bennington is born.

DESTROYER

THE SESSIONS

What's particularly amusing about the construction of the *Destroyer* album is that the band indeed cooked up a whole load of songs, and then producer Ezrin unceremoniously rejected all of them, save for "God of Thunder," "King of the Night Time World," and "Detroit Rock City," which would, of course, dominate the album. Fully fifteen demo songs were recorded in August 1975 at Magna Graphics Studio, pertinently without Ezrin, and it was slim pickings.

"Doncha Hesitate" was a typical Bachman-Turner Overdrive–like boogie rocker, sung by Paul, worthy of being a deep track on *Dressed to Kill* but nothing more. Paul also sang on the original "God of Thunder" arrangement, which was faster and propelled by a bit of a disco beat, given Peter's double-fisted sixteenth-note high hat work. "It's the Fire" was Stonesy and similar to "Doncha Hesitate" and a half dozen songs from the original trio of albums. Paul's original "Detroit Rock City" demo leaned harder on the song's iconic riff and less so on hanging chords. It's a bit of a knees-up party shuffle, like Slade at their heaviest. The final track of the Paul tranche, "Love Is Alright," sounded like a lost and exhausted version of "Rock Bottom." All told, there was a true demo feel here, where you can hear the wheels turning, imagining that Paul was working out if any of these parts are worth keeping and maybe chucking into another song.

Peter was a bit of a mess at the time, and Ace was unproductive as well. The Catman talked about being deep into the cocaine during this period but also working super-hard on his drum parts (Ezrin is practically apologetic for what he put Peter through, but he is also proud to say that, contrary to rumors, Peter was the only drummer on *Destroyer*). Ace was similarly shocked at how hard of a taskmaster Ezrin was. In the end, the Spaceman would not be there for important sessions and show up as a cowriter on but a single track, "Flaming Youth."

As Paul told me when asked if it was a less-than-ideal situation with Ace and Peter, "Ideal has to do with compatibility, but it also has a lot to do with combustibility. Ideal doesn't necessarily mean smooth. Certainly, in the beginning, what helped create Kiss was this, I guess, disparity and the divergence of opinions. The only thing that needed to be harnessed, always, were those talents and those personalities. And that took the two more disciplined people to do."

Fortunately, the songwriting, at least from Paul and Gene, was there in both quality and quantity.

"I've known since day one, the songs were great," reflects Paul, again from my same chat with him in 2005. "The fact that the vast majority of those songs were written on acoustic guitars,

IN MUSIC NEWS ...

In March '76, Kiss competitors on different ends of the spectrum, the Bay City Rollers and Rush, issue hit albums, *Rock n' Roll Love Letter* and *2112*, respectively, both of which will certify gold in America in 1977. The Bay City Rollers album reaches No. 1 in Canada, as does its cloying single, "Money Honey," whereas the Rush album yields no hits.

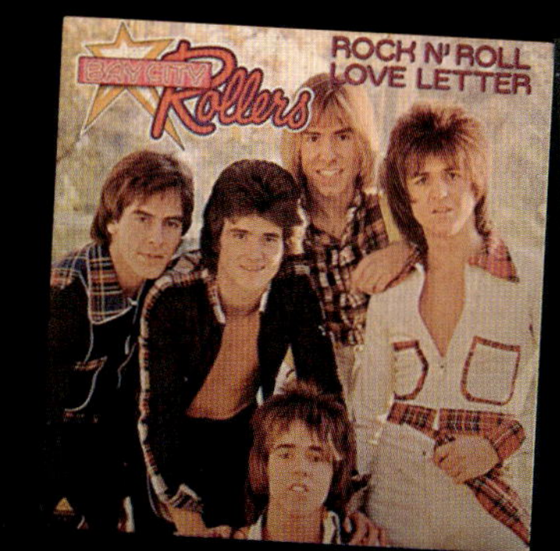

Kiss rocks the Calderone Theater in Hempstead, New York, on August 24, 1975. The band recorded fifteen demos that month for the album that would become *Destroyer.*

without an amplifier, without a smoke bomb, without a flash pot or a fog machine, they're good songs. They can be played on a single guitar and they're catchy. And it's always ironic to me that all the bands that all the critics in the beginning thought were incredible, sound terribly dated today. Our first few albums sound like what people still aspire to and copy. Someone else was saying to me a couple days ago, when I sit around . . . another producer friend of mine said that one of his best memories was he and I sitting in a stairwell in a recording studio during a Kiss session, and I'm just playing acoustic guitar. So there is a power to those songs that perhaps gets a little, if not lost, sidetracked, when you're overwhelmed with everything else that goes into Kiss."

Also concerning the songs, Gene generated ten demos for possible inclusion. "Bad, Bad Lovin'" would morph into *Rock and Roll Over*'s "Calling Dr. Love." Then there's "Man of a Thousand Faces," which one can imagine as a *Destroyer* track, given its thoughtful vibe, its topical lyric, and general Ezrin-ness. It would show up on Gene's solo album in 1978. "I Don't Want No Romance" is basically a wet noodle version of "Ladies Room," to appear on *Rock and Roll Over*, and "Burnin' Up with Fever" is hard funk like Aerosmith (say, "Last Child") to keep it contemporary, while "Rock n' Rolls Royce" is another one that would show up, transformed on *Rock and Roll Over*—part "See You in Your Dreams" and part "Love 'Em and Leave 'Em."

Then there's "Mad Dog," which would generate an incidental riff used as part of "Flaming Youth," along with some lyrics for "Sweet Pain." In the main, though, it's galumphing funk like Moxy or, again,

Also doing well and somewhat seen as Kiss competitors at the time, at least for the attentions of a female demographic, are ABBA, who begin an Australian promotional campaign on March 4. Donna Summer issues *A Love Trilogy* on March 5, helping Casablanca keep the lights on, and March 6 sees the rerelease of twenty-two Beatles

singles. Are Kiss the Beatles of the 1970s? Likely not. However, after the Fab Four, Kiss and Led Zeppelin represent, arguably, the two next most influential bands on the careers of future rockers.

Then there's the Who, another storied institution. On March 9, drummer Keith Moon collapses in concert at the Boston Garden.

Also in March, the Sensational Alex Harvey Band issues their fifth album, *The Penthouse Tapes*. Not exactly competition for Kiss, they deserve a mention because guitarist Zal Cleminson is known for his "mime" makeup. Zal would eventually wind up in Nazareth but imagine what Kiss might have sounded like with Cleminson in the

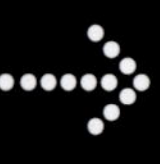

Ace later expressed surprise at how hard Ezrin worked the band. In the end, Ace's only cowrite on the album would be "Flaming Youth," the album's second single.

band. Incidentally, the *Bricks* album by Hello People, issued in 1975, showed the whole band in black-and-white makeup. The move was purely mime, which was a part of the band's narrative going back to its inception in 1967.

Speaking of Nazareth, in March the hard-drinking Scots issue *Close Enough for Rock 'n' Roll*, followed by

Playin' the Game later in the year. But the band's bold and boisterous music is from their previous four albums, and due to the band's creative choices, they won't compete much with Aerosmith, Kiss, or Ted Nugent past 1975's *Hair of the Dog.*

The March issue of *Creem* features four pages of Kiss koverage, written by Robert Duncan, as well as

On the other end of the production spectrum from Ace, Gene produced ten demos for *Destroyer*.

the results of the 1975 readers' poll, in which Kiss are voted fifth-best group and *Alive!* is voted fifth-best album (and also fifth-best album cover). Kiss also take second place as a live act, after the Rolling Stones, and second place as worst group, after the Bay City Rollers.

On March 16, the day after *Destroyer* shows up in record (and head) shops,

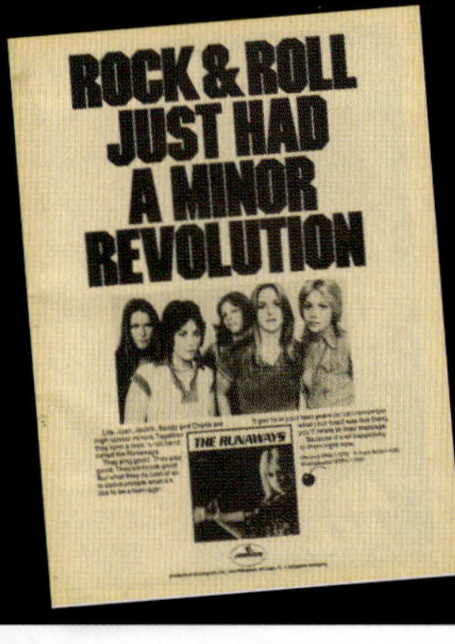

the *Runaways* issue their self-titled debut. Young Kiss fans who are aware of the band (not difficult, given substantial coverage in *Circus* and *Creem*) embrace them as the female version of Kiss. As David McGee writes in his *Rolling Stone* review of the album, "What's a joker to make of such a product, rife as it is with warmed-over Kiss and Sweet licks?"

On March 19, Paul Kossoff, Back Street Crawler and ex-Free, dies on an airplane due to complications from drugs he'd taken. As previously mentioned, his band had just supported Kiss. The next day, Alice Cooper marries Sheryl Goddard, a happy union that persists to this day. March 26, Thin Lizzy issue their impressive *Jailbreak*

Aerosmith. Next among Gene's demos is "Night Boy," also funk but more up-tempo, with a tricky off-kilter rhythmic counterbalance. "Star" is sparse and experimental, but it's got good bones—this could have been turned into a strident rocker, a centerpiece perhaps not on *Destroyer* but certainly on *Rock and Roll Over*. "Howlin' for Your Love" is yet another hummable boogie-rocking pop number, demonstrating Kiss's connection to the British blues boom as filtered through the MC5, Mitch Ryder, and the Amboy Dukes. Finally there's "True Confessions," which is sturdy enough to have fit on *Destroyer*. It's another one that would emerge on Gene's first solo album, featuring background vocals by Helen Reddy.

The first actual recording sessions with Ezrin took place September 3–6 at Electric Lady Studios, with the *Alive!* album due for release on September 10, meaning that this was an act still fully in desperation mode and looking for answers. Ezrin, having worked magic for Alice Cooper, would be able to provide those answers despite some skepticism from the band, who really wanted Eddie Kramer to produce the album or, failing that, Jimmy Ienner, who'd done all the Raspberries albums and some recent records for Three Dog Night.

When asked whether there had been pressure on Kiss to come up with a hit single at this juncture, Ezrin said: "I'm sure there was. There is always pressure on everybody to try and succeed. I'd met them in Toronto in a stairwell at City Television, which is well documented. But I had basically heard about them from a kid in Toronto named Mike, who called me up, used to call my home phone, because I was listed in those days. He would call my home phone and talk to me about what was cool and what was not. And he said one day, 'There is this band you ought to produce one day; they're called Kiss. They are amazing, but the records are not amazing. They should have you as a producer.' And I said, 'Thank you Mike; that's really sweet.'

That was that, and then three weeks later I found myself in the stairwell with them at City Television. I was going down as they were coming up the stairs to be interviewed. They wanted better. But I don't know; it wasn't "You guys better come up with a hit single and therefore you oughta go get this guy." I think everybody was just feeling that they were much better live than they were on record, and that they needed something extra to sort of push them over. And as it turns out, their live album captured them better than their studio album, and that was the first bit of success that they had before *Destroyer*. And then *Destroyer* came out, and I wasn't thinking the whole time, What's a single and what's not a single? I was just thinking, What's a great rock song? And of course, trying to make it radio-friendly as much as possible, keeping my intros short, and keeping it within the three minutes the radio was demanding in those days, stuff like that.

album featuring "The Boys Are Back in Town," Kiss-like and an enduring classic. Also on this impressive day in the record business, Judas Priest issue their groundbreaking heavy metal masterpiece *Sad Wings of Destiny*, followed a week later by *Presence* from Led Zeppelin. The former represents a baby band in

"But the mandate wasn't, 'Go make hit singles.' The mandate was, 'Go cut a great album.' Cut a great album that shows this band off for what they are. And my philosophy at the time—and it's still true now—is that the recording is just sound. And when people see a band and experience them, they have all these other senses at work at the same time. And then when they put on a recording, they wonder why it isn't as exciting. And it's not as exciting because the recording only captures one component of what they experienced. And so in order to compensate, my approach for production has always been, the recording has got to be larger or more dramatic than life. It's either larger or smaller, more intimate, more grand, whatever it is. More dramatic than reality."

In hiring Ezrin, there might have been the thought that a bunch of zesty, delightful sound-picture things had been done for shock rocker Alice Cooper and maybe he could do the same thing to spruce up a Kiss that wasn't catching. Ezrin agreed: "Yeah, I'm sure there was a little bit of that. But there's also, when you get a rock-and-roller . . . for the most part, scratch a heavy rocker, and underneath he's a marshmallow who likes Broadway musicals (laughs). There is that, right? That's in both Gene and Paul, but in particular, Gene, who didn't get to the United States until he was in his early teens and learned English from television. They were children of the media. They were moved by the same things I was moved by: movies and television and science fiction and comic books and all that sort of stuff that is imaginative, boyish, fantastical stuff. So we just brought it into the record."

Besides bringing the thoughtful conceptual stuff, Ezrin was also an excellent communicator of his ideas, as Gene attests. Gene also remembers Ezrin teaching them about harmonic tuning and generally being impressed at how much they were learning from him about music theory, about discipline, and yes, about making something theatrical and conceptual. Paul soaked it all in as well, relishing the opportunity to learn from Ezrin, who would teach them about time signatures and double-tracking, with either guitars or piano. He recalled fondly that Ezrin would wear a whistle around his neck and call the band "campers," hollering at them to get back to work. He called the experience "musical boot camp."

The September sessions resulted in a little less than half of the basic working tracks. The second and final tranche of dates to finish the record would take place mostly in January and into February at the Record Plant, separated out partly because Kiss was in dispute with Casablanca, with other labels making offers to steal the band away from Bogart. But by this point, *Alive!* was blowing up and there was excitement about the band's prospects. Simultaneously, they felt a sense of loyalty to Casablanca, given everything they'd gone through with Bogart to get this far.

This is when Ezrin untethered the band from the past and introduced all manner of ear candy, from backward recordings to choirs and classical ensemble work, soundtrack bits and the car crash used in "Detroit Rock City." This is despite having been limited to sixteen tracks, resulting in multiple parts having to go on at the same time. One interesting wrinkle inside of the January sessions concerns a track that Ezrin had brought in called "Ain't None of Your Business," written by Becky Hobbs and Lew Anderson. It's distinguished by having been significantly professionally recorded, in contrast to the collection of demos. What's more, it's a fully viable track, featuring a smart chord sequence, a slow but intriguing pace, and Peter on surly vocals. In the end, despite the song not making the album, there would be a measured degree of outside songwriting and even guest performances, namely Alice Cooper solo band guitarist Dick Wagner, called in because Ace was being uncooperative.

As Ace wrote in his autobiography, *No Regrets*: "It's long been a suggested that studio guitar players were brought in to help out on *Destroyer*, filling in for me on the days when I simply wasn't there. Well, the truth is that it happened a few times. I can't deny it. Most of the guitar work on *Destroyer* is mine, but not all of it. I was hitting the clubs a lot at night in those days, living the life of a rock star. Sometimes that lifestyle wasn't particularly conducive to making a record. I was starting to get out of control, but I probably would have been a lot more cognizant, and I would have showed up more and been on time, if I had gotten more encouragement from Gene, Paul, and Bob. But it wasn't my record. In fact, of all the Kiss records to that point, *Destroyer* felt the least like my record. It belonged more to Paul and Gene, and to Bob."

astonishing ascendance; the latter is a storied institution in decline.

Priest's much lauded leather-and-studs heavy metal uniform came together with the *Unleashed in the East* live album in time for the New Wave of British Heavy Metal . . . it looked a lot like what Kiss had been wearing for years.

This page and following: Kiss brings their spectacle to Assembly Center in Tulsa, Oklahoma, on March 8.

Paul's demo version of "Detroit Rock City" leaned harder on the song's iconic riff and less so on hanging chords.

***Destroyer* and *Love Gun* cover artist Ken Kelly, pictured at the New Jersey Horror Con & Film Festival on March 2, 2018.**

THE ALBUM COVER

Naturally, Kiss (notably Gene) wanted Frank Frazetta to do the *Destroyer* album cover, but the fantasy art legend turned out to be too pricey and also wouldn't allow Kiss to use the image beyond the album cover. But there was Ken Kelly, who was a relative to Frank by marriage—Frank's wife, Ellie, was Ken's aunt. Fortunately, Kelly had already been doing horror-styled illustration, and according to Peter's wife Lydia, it was Peter who had been reading *Eerie* and *Creepy* magazine and who had noticed Kelly, who had also worked for *Castle of Frankenstein* magazine in the early 1970s and generally was one of the most prolific artists for James Warren and Warren Publications. For his part, Casablanca art director Dennis Woloch said that after getting nowhere with Frazetta, he had gone to a comic book store and spotted Kelly's work on a cover of *Creepy*, specifically an illustration of a robot.

"They were—and are—larger than life," remarked Kelly, after seeing the band at a New York meet-and-greet in full makeup and costume. Kelly knew nothing of the band's music, having more conservative tastes. He'd just gotten out of the Marine Corps, and the world of glam rock was a shock to say the least, much less what the band members were wearing.

In any event, he was sufficiently inspired. The brief from the band and Woloch was that the band should be depicted four abreast, leaping at the viewer with fire behind them. Given a thirty-day deadline and working in oil paint using photo slides as reference, the first version he did for the band was deemed too violent by the label. As well, it incorporated the costumes from the *Alive!* tour and thus would look out of date. (It can be seen in all its fiery, apocalyptic glory as the front cover of the album in remixed form circa 2012.) The final, more purple-tinged image isn't much different, although the scene behind the band looks marginally less in flames, perhaps smokier, mixed with the effects of a dust storm. According to manager Bill Aucoin, Kelly took the request for a makeover cheerfully and in stride, even after almost finishing a less destructive version, only to be told it had to be changed again because of the costume issue. Kelly did not do the lettering.

Amusingly, the back cover art is pretty much as violent as anything that Casablanca rejected—it's basically a city being ravaged by a massive conflagration. Of note, moving to the inner sleeve of the album, which has nothing to do with Kelly, there's the all-important call to "join the Kiss Army." One sees the nifty new Kiss Army emblem, above which are instructions to "SHOUT IT OUT LOUD." On the reverse are the lyrics to one song, "Detroit Rock City," which, like with Led Zeppelin before them ("Stairway to Heaven"), tends to mark that song as important, possibly even a work of high art.

Kelly passed away at the age of seventy-six on June 2, 2022, but his art lives on—sort of. Before his death, Kelly commented that he thinks Gene owns the original painting he did for *Destroyer*, but the official version used in 1976 was lost in a fire. Kelly would be called back to do the *Love Gun* cover, and that one for sure lives on, having changed hands at auction. As (handsomely paid) work-for-hire jobs, neither cover resulted in any royalties for Kelly.

The cultural reach of *Destroyer* has been such that a 1999 feature film used a Kiss concert (albeit set in 1978) as its organizing principle—and borrowed "Detroit Rock City" as its own title.

TRACK BY TRACK

Don't believe today's narrative on *Destroyer*—or Paul's or Ezrin's. It was, for the most part, well received and only maligned here and there. Or put it this way: It was partly maligned quite thoroughly, specifically for "Beth" and "Great Expectations." In any event, here's a blow-by-blow look at the record that by consensus (and not strong consensus, mind you) is seen as the pinnacle of the band's catalog.

"Detroit Rock City"

Speaking of consensus, another popular one is that "Detroit Rock City" is pretty much the best song Kiss ever wrote. As Paul tells it, Ezrin implored the band to write about something other than sex, at which point Paul recalled that he had heard that a fan had been killed in a car crash on the way to a Kiss concert, possibly in Charlotte, North Carolina. He grafted that idea and the underlying reflection on how life can change on a dime onto this song he had about Detroit.

As for the Pink Floyd–like soundtrack bit at the beginning, this was something fresh for Kiss. One envisions a Kiss fan at home washing the dishes and watching the news on TV about a car accident. He then leaves, gets into his own (presumably muscle) car, and pops some Kiss into his car stereo, namely "Rock and Roll All Nite." The news anchor is, in fact, Ezrin, and the dishes effect is there because he did it washing dishes in the studio bathroom, after which he compressed and EQ'd his voice so it sounded like it was coming from the idiot box. Engineer Corky Stasiak is part of the process as well, jingling his keys, humming along to the song, and revving the engine, not from a muscle car but rather his Toyota SR5 pickup, parked outside. The snippet of "Rock and Roll All Nite" heard from the *Alive!* album was done for real as well, played on the cassette deck in Stasiak's truck.

Next comes the iconic, dramatic riff, with guitar doubled by piano—and off into the song's majestic lingering power chords. Distinguishing the song further is Gene's busy, full-frontal bass line, which wasn't on Paul's original demo. Gene quite rightly says it's nontypical for him, quite R&B and similar to Isaac Hayes's "Theme from *Shaft*." He also credits Ezrin for coming up with it. Later, again, adding gravitas, there's a flamenco-inspired solo that was conceived by Ezrin as a tension-builder and then coaxed out of Ace. Ezrin had Peter playing to a click track, a process that Peter found frustrating, admitting to his "wild" sense of timing. As for his swirling, swinging part, Peter says it was a collaboration between Paul, Ezrin, and him.

All told, "Detroit Rock City" is an accomplished and modern heavy metal song with interesting chords, a gloriously anthemic chorus, and a relatively complex break section, accompanied by throaty engine revs. At the end, Paul utters the thoughts of the doomed driver, there's a false ending and more chorus and twin leads, followed by a gut-wrenching skid and loud, shocking crash.

Amusingly, Paul has revealed that the reason the minute-and-a-half intro sequence exists at all is that the band was worried that the album was coming up a little short. In the end, quite symmetrically, *Destroyer* starts with this cinematic passage and then closes with the haunting sequence at the conclusion of "Do You Love Me," separated out in later years with the title "Rock 'n' Roll Party."

The Catman performs for 9,000 fans at the Assembly Center, Tulsa, Oklahoma, March 8, 1976.

"King of the Night Time World"

"King of the Night Time World" begins as one of the few songs rescued from the Magna Graphic demo sessions. But it has a history before this, having been written by Mark Anthony from the Hollywood Stars and destined for an album in 1974 that got shelved. (It's since been released, and the glossy, finished production of the song comes off more like the Rolling Stones of the adjacent *It's Only Rock 'n' Roll* era.) This echoed an earlier situation, when that band's song "Escape," produced by Ezrin, was recycled for Alice Cooper's *Welcome to My Nightmare* album. In fact, it was Ezrin who went back to the band and asked them about "King of the Night Time World," which was then given to Paul to work up in demo form.

As the band's manager Kim Fowley explained to me, "'King of the Night Time World' I cowrote, and then the guys in Kiss later reworked it. And then while at Kiss, I did 'Do You Love Me.' Those are staples in heavy metal diets. When I met Kiss, they were certainly influenced by Slade. But Gene and Paul are PhDs of music; those guys are real smart. And then so is Alice Cooper. They had Ezrin from Toronto, who's a genius, who, at the time, looked like Al Pacino in *The Godfather*. So, he was almost a movie star-looking engineer. He probably looks like a grandfather now."

Fowley, who deserves credit for some of the lyrics, added, "When I went to work as their cowriter, I asked Gene, 'What's the gimmick?' And he said, 'The concept, Kim, is Halloween. And leather and *Rocky Horror Picture Show* and midnight movie crowds minus the gay element. We wanted to call ourselves Fuck, but our manager wouldn't let us—so we became Kiss, the next best thing.'"

"King of the Night Time World" is all that and more, a testimony to the band's life philosophy and in particular Paul's, according to Paul himself. Also adding substance and dynamic is the nonobvious arrangement, beginning with a verse where there's no bass guitar and then adding that the next time around, although, still oddly, there's only sort of high, incidental, boogie rock guitars. In other words, it still doesn't feel like there's a bottom end at the verses, keeping the experience buoyant, literally. Elsewhere, there's the strangeness of Peter's military snare beat, which anchors the chorus, contrasting the liftoff effect we get from the verse. There's also memorable—albeit slight—twin lead work and a chest-thumping run at the chorus, which raises the stakes on what is already an anthemic tagline in the repeated title.

The King of the Night Time World plays guitar between his legs at Richfield Coliseum outside Cleveland, Ohio.

Ace in the dressing room at The Forum, Inglewood, California. Note the bottle of Mateus in the foreground—it was the hit wine of the day, available in rosé and white.

"God of Thunder"

"God of Thunder" is another one that survived the ruthless demo cull, only it originated with Paul and then got transferred over to Gene, who embodied the character described in the lyric better. Paul remembers being stunned when Ezrin nonchalantly said that they should slow it down and have Gene sing it. In hindsight, he recognized that Ezrin was right, because "God of Thunder" became Gene's signature song, his primary calling card from the entire catalog. Live, it became the place in the show where Gene might spit blood, do a bass solo, or be vaulted into the air and over the crowd.

Those are Ezrin's kids you hear at the beginning, four and nine, running around with walkie-talkies and space helmets playing chase the monster, lending a haunting quality to what is already murky and doomy, an effect underscored by the whooshing wind sounds.

What's brilliant about "God of Thunder" is how intentioned it was on the part of Ezrin to slow the song down and utilize a sort of caveman drum part for it. The idea was to present as many rhythms, tempos, and time signatures as possible across the landscape of the album, as well as numerous keys and writing styles, not to mention provide liberal use of ear candy. Gene's vocal is thick and menacing, and for the cacophonous break section, pounded by drums and swirled with scary sound effects (and a return of Ezrin's kids), Ezrin had Peter record in an elevator shaft, where he began playing and was surprised by two sanitation workers who came in to take away the garbage.

In the end, "God of Thunder," with its "rob you of your virgin soul" talk and Gene declaring, "I was raised by the demons," is about as evil as Kiss ever got, enough to put them in the little black books of evangelical preachers, who started calling the band Kings in Satan's Service.

"Great Expectations"

As expected, at thirteen years old (actually a month shy of it), I recall a sense of revulsion upon first hearing "Great Expectations," although now I quite fancy it, while I still don't like anything about "Beth." But even then, there was also the recognition that they'd gone too far, and by "they," I mean the band members—I don't remember even thinking about the producer at the time. A mental note was made that clearly there were textures on the song that didn't come from a four-piece hard rock band. In other words, I was reminded of *Welcome to My Nightmare*, which, as it turned out, was also produced by Ezrin, whatever that meant. There was also a sense of "You Can't Always Get What You Want" by the Rolling Stones in it when it came to the vaulted, churchy chorus of this incendiary shocker of a song, provided by the Brooklyn Boys Choir.

Written on bass, "Great Expectations" originates with Gene as something called "I Am a New Man," which he framed as English and ethereal. Gene had originally written the Kiss band members' names into the song, but Ezrin talked him out of that, emphasizing that it should be more universal. As for the evolving lyric, Gene really was influenced by the 1946 film version of Charles Dickens's novel *Great Expectations*. Once Ezrin heard it, he decided to give the song a George Martin treatment, although there's Phil Spector in there as well, plus an admitted lift from Beethoven's "Sonata Pathétique." With respect to the final lyric and its gaudy musical backing, Ezrin perceived it to be as autobiographical for Gene as "God of Thunder" was but more of a parody of what he represented as a rock star, namely over-the-top, serious but not serious, in the spirit of what Paul would often say of himself: "I'm not a ham; I'm the whole pig."

Gene spills some (stage) blood for his Los Angeles fans.

"Flaming Youth"

Flip over the original vinyl (on your parents' wooden stereo console unit, which might include the TV), and one encounters the first of fully four *Destroyer* tracks connectable to the oeuvre of the original trio of studio albums.

"Flaming Youth" represents Ace's only writing credit on the album, sharing it with Paul, Gene, and Ezrin, but he's yet to step up to the mic and do a lead vocal on a Kiss album. Ace told me: "I don't even consider myself a singer. I basically sing because I have to (laughs). If I didn't have to sing, I probably wouldn't sing as much. I would rather have a singer like Robert Plant from Led Zeppelin. I would rather have him do the majority of the singing, and I would focus on all the guitar work. I consider myself a songwriter/guitar player. But yeah, the singing is fun.

"I thought everybody had a unique voice and very distinctive. When you hear my voice, or Peter Criss's voice, or Paul Stanley's voice, you could immediately tell the difference. It's not like, 'Wow, is this this guy or that guy?' Pete has that scratchy voice, and mine is sort of more middle-of-the-road, maybe a little higher. Paul's got a really strong voice, and he's a great songwriter. Basically there's a lot of flexibility in the group because we did the three- and four-part harmonies, and that freed us up to write stuff that was a little more intricate vocally, than maybe some other bands would. I think it just added another dimension to Kiss."

On the subject of dovetailing guitar-wise with Paul, Ace says, "I worked well with Paul. I used to try and complement his rhythm parts with octave rhythm parts. He was giving me free rein to do interesting guitar solos on top of the songs that he wrote. He was always a really good songwriter, and I enjoyed working with Paul."

It's Paul that sings this very direct youth anthem, very quickly setting a scene where the parents don't understand the kids. It recalls "I'm Eighteen" by Alice Cooper, from the album that marked Ezrin's first project with the band. It also sounds like a contemporary Alice Cooper song, similar to "Escape" and "Department of Youth" from *Welcome to My Nightmare*. Ezrin pieced this song together from parts the band had and added the controversial calliope part in the chorus, which again, circus-like, gave the song an Alice Cooper solo-years vibe, although it was the Beatles Ezrin was going for. The band didn't think it was necessary, and Ezrin indeed has expressed regret over it. Note also how the snare whacks are removed from the chorus, giving it a subdued, crouched effect, a sense of contrast to the other parts with bigger beats.

As alluded to, one section of "Flaming Youth," sort of the post-chorus, was brought forward from a song called "Mad Dog." As for the title, Kiss had opened for a band called Flaming Youth back in the early days, and once Ezrin heard that, he thought it was a great title for a song—it seems fanciful, but numerous times in interviews I've had rock stars tell me a song concept, and subsequently a whole bank of lyrics was generated by nothing more than a promising song title.

"Flaming Youth" is the first of three tracks featuring Alice Cooper solo band cowriter Dick Wagner on guitar, with Wagner doing the screeching licks in the outro. Wagner says: "I played acoustic guitar on 'Beth' and the lead solo on 'Sweet Pain,' and I think I played on one or two other songs, but I can't remember. I was living in New York, and they needed me to come in and do something. I was available for sessions for everybody at that time. I did a lot of sessions, so there I was. I got along well with Paul and Gene, and Ace wasn't around, so I was doing whatever he was supposed to do. I was basically called in as a studio musician to come in and play my parts. There wasn't really any involvement in the writing."

When asked about Cooper's views on Kiss, Wagner answers: "I think he always thought they were a derivative of his work. I think that he's probably right, except that Kiss was very original. They may not have been original by doing makeup and all that; Alice was definitely the guy who started that. They were original from a different whole point of view. They appeal to their audience in a different way than Alice Cooper ever did. They made themselves into a larger-than-life band. Alice was a little more intellectual. I don't know exactly how to describe it, but there was definitely a cerebral thing going on, even though the kids were into it because of the pure rock 'n' roll of it."

"Sweet Pain"

"Sweet Pain" is the second track that would have fit anywhere on the first three albums, most pertinently *Dressed to Kill*, given the overlaying of acoustic guitar onto the primary-colored power chords. This one's primarily from Gene, who calls it an "S&M pop song." Mathematically, one might call the chorus (hard, loud) pop, but it's made Kiss-able by the verses, which are heavy metal enough.

This song represents Wagner's biggest contribution to the album, although it's little more than a brief guitar solo. As Gene recalls, with the band in ascendance, Ace was starting to hang around with the wrong people. Whether it was clubbing at Studio 54 or "being late for a card game," Ace wasn't around—and the irked band wanted to keep on schedule. One must also remember that Ezrin was into the substances, too, doing coke just like Peter. But with those two, it was actually helping them get the work done. Ace, on the other hand, was usually sluggish from what he was taking, beginning what Gene called a thirty-five-year slide.

Comparing the two guitar solos, Wagner's sounds very much like what Ace might do, choppy and spirited, while Ace's, heard on the *Resurrected* version of the album, doesn't sound like Ace at all, being a tight bit of composing, a song within a song. Ace's solo was actually laid down before Wagner's, but the band wasn't entirely happy with it. This is why Ace's performance is called the original solo on *Resurrected*. Ace flipped out when he heard what had happened, but by that point, there was nothing he could do.

As for the song itself, Gene says it originated with a demo of his called "Rock n' Rolls Royce," although there's more of that song's characteristics across two songs on *Rock and Roll Over*. Gene has also indicated that it was inspired by "Wild Thing" by the Troggs, especially at the vocal end.

Ace breaks out his beloved smoking guitar gag.

"Shout It Out Loud"

Wrote *Record World* on March 20, 1975, "A preview of things to come from their *Destroyer* LP, this track shows the group becoming more musical without losing any of the raw edge that has become their trademark. A worthy follow to 'Rock and Roll All Nite.'" Indeed "Shout It Out Loud" would be issued as *Destroyer*'s first single, and both the verse and the sweeter chorus would sound crashing and triumphant like the band's first anthem, modestly performing on radio at this juncture.

The idea for "Shout It Out Loud" originates with a Hollies song called "I Wanna Shout," from the band's tenth album, *Confessions of the Mind*. Gene and his old band Wicked Lester covered it, actually properly recording it, but as "We Wanna Shout It Out Loud," which is what is sung in the chorus of the Hollies song. A variation of this is what Gene started singing as he and Paul and Ezrin sat at the piano in Ezrin's apartment on Fifty-Second Street in New York one morning, and the song was born inside of half an hour. Ezrin remembers fondly that writing with the guys was something rather uncommon, given that the usual process was that Paul and Gene would write and record demos on their own. He also recalls being inspired by the song's descending bass line, while Gene found inspiration in the idea of shouting out whatever your mission might be, recognizing that the Hollies song was about something very different, more about having to keep a relationship secret while wanting to tell the world.

As Paul explains, the call-and-response vocal in the uplifting chorus was inspired by a similar technique regularly used by the Four Tops, with Peter also citing the Four Tops for the drumbeat, namely "I Can't Help Myself," aka "I Can't Help Myself (Sugar Pie, Honey Bunch)." There's not much similarity, other than a bit in the chorus plus, throughout, the use of tambourine, which is rendered more subtle on the Kiss track, possibly combined with shakers.

"Beth"

"Beth" begins as a song that Peter and Stan Penridge had back in the Chelsea days (but not on the band's album) called "Beck," about guitarist Mike Brand's wife, Becky, constantly calling the band when they were trying to rehearse. Peter hummed it to Gene one day in the back of a limo, and Gene suggested using the name Beth instead (so fans didn't think it was about Jeff Beck!). He also suggested showing the song to Ezrin.

Picking up the story, Ezrin told me: "We had to do a Peter Criss song. That was the political thing. You know, Peter had to have one song on the record, and selecting, and in many cases cowriting the material for the rest of the album. Peter came in with a bunch of possibilities and nothing struck me except for this song called 'Beck.' It was sort of country or folk feeling. I can't honestly remember the original lyric, but it wasn't about this, the woman waiting for him at home and he loves her to death and finally choosing his music over the relationship. It was about making his music, and the process of romance. It was a romantic song.

"And the whole idea behind the orchestra and the piano part and all that sort of stuff, I mean, I wrote that piano part and actually rewrote the song. This was not presented to me as a piano ballad. I made it a piano ballad. It came in as a folk-rock song, with guitars and bass and drums, and it was faster. I took the song home and rewrote it and brought it back as 'Beth,' and doing things like, 'Our house just ain't a home,' and you're sort of broken-hearted. It's actually very sweet and very innocent and kind of a confessional song. For me it became the ballad on the record. I always like to have a ballad on the record, if for no other reason than to break up the action. So, you had something that wasn't pounding you over the head the whole time. So, it became the big ballad for me, and of course the minute that we cut it, I knew it was a hit. But nobody in the band really wanted to deal with it."

(And as the story goes . . .) "Detroit Rock City" was the A-side, with "Beth" on the B-side, and some smart DJ flipped it and said, "Screw that; I like this one," and started to play it. These were the days when DJs could play the records they liked. And it caused such a reaction that the whole station went on it, and the region went on it, and then the country went on it, and then it went Top Ten.

Indeed the song is a piano ballad, but Wagner plays some acoustic guitar on it, which you can hear more of on the *Resurrected* version. As well there's full-on orchestration, provided by H.A. MacMillan and the New York Philharmonic Orchestra.

As for how "Beth" changed the complexion of Kiss's fan base, Ezrin says: "There were more girls. And that was absolutely intentional on my part. I did go into this project having seen the band live, and I completely got it. I had this visceral understanding of what it was they needed to accomplish.

"We actually had a meeting in a restaurant in New York before we ever started where I told them, you know, right now you guys appeal to pimply fifteen-year-old boys and that's it. That's a limited audience, and there's only so far you're going to be able to go with this. But you're not really sexy. You're not really touching girls or cool guys or any of that sort of stuff. You're just touching the outcasts. And that's kind of okay as a jumping-off point, but that can't be the end-all and be-all. What I said to them was, you can still be the monsters and . . . these characters, but we have to inject a little bit of vulnerability and lovability into it.

"And I used as an example the film *The Wild One*, with Marlon Brando. I said, Johnny was a biker and a bad guy and everything that society was against—parents hated him. But the girls just felt the need to want to take care of him and cuddle him and love him and try to civilize him. And I said that's what we have to bring into Kiss. There has to be a crack in the armor, and you have to have a certain amount of vulnerability. Girls are going to need to want to reach out and love you and bring you in, you know, take care of you and rehabilitate you, or whatever the word is.

"And so we needed to find material that was sexier, and we needed to find material that couldn't just be full-on cocks and balls all the time. I told them, if you walk into a room and you start swinging your dick, people run for the exits. But if you can gently walk up to someone and begin to stroke them and talk them into bed, that's what we've got to be doing on this record.

"So, everybody was excited by that idea. They thought I knew something they didn't know. They were excited by that, and that's how we began the project. Looking for that sort of stuff. So, we wrote things like 'Do You Love Me,' which was absolutely right down that center. You know, it's kind of cocky, but it's Johnny from *The Wild One*. It's cocky, but underneath it all it's insecure and, 'Do you really love me?' And 'Beth' really solved the problem, because by being the first big hit, it opens up a whole new look for these guys. It's, 'Me and the boys will be playing all night,' and then you can go off and be cocky again."

The Kiss Army gets some prominent stage placement.

"Do You Love Me"

Like many songs on *Destroyer*, "Do You Love Me" is effortlessly accessible despite novel construction. It begins with boomy drums, after which Paul sings a verse but with no music besides drums. Then it goes into the hypnotic, lingering chords of the chorus, placed upon Chapman/Chinn UK glam drums, followed by a satisfying collapse into another verse, this time with everybody playing and, in particular, the bass part carrying the melody, or more accurately, guitars, bass, and vocals dovetailing expertly, each providing an independent melody.

As the mercurial and anarchic Kim Fowley has alluded to, he had a significant hand in the writing of this song and thus garners one-third credit. Paul loves the song for its attitude, along with the break section, where you get some twin leads, higher-register singing, tubular bells, and modulation. Then it's back to seemingly endless repetitions of the chorus, where interest is maintained by sort of girl-group backing vocals, little gasping interjections, and an almost Phil Spector–like arrangement that sounds like Christmas music. My own impression upon first hearing the song in 1976—and that has held forevermore—is that it's weirdly incomplete but still satisfying, almost an instrumental but with vocals, virtually all chorus.

Another impression upon first hearing it is that the closing sound collage on the album, later named "Rock 'n' Roll Party" and actually missing from some pressings of the album, was indeed part of the song, giving it an extra layer of menace. Synthesizers strafe the landscape, while churchy voices reverberate like angels and demons and witches. Halfway through, they coalesce around the chorus of "Great Expectations," simultaneous with Paul doing his *Alive!* "Looks like we're gonna have ourselves a rock 'n' roll party" spiel, on loop, on fade. Pretty creepy.

The Statistics

The lead single from *Destroyer*, "Shout It Out Loud," achieved a #31 placement on the *Billboard* charts but also #1 in Canada. It spent ten weeks on the *Billboard* grid in total. The live version from October 1977's *Alive II* (further linking the song to the "Rock and Roll All Nite" narrative, with a studio version and live version both out as singles), got to #54 in the United States and #74 in Canada.

The second single from the album, "Flaming Youth," stalled at #74 in the United States and #73 in Canada, lasting only three weeks on *Billboard*. Distinguishing the release was its picture sleeve presentation, plus the fact that it was the first Kiss single to feature the new tan "Casbah" Casablanca label as opposed to the old blue "smoking man" one. Third single "Detroit Rock City" failed to chart in the United States, despite its deep edit, but "Beth" reversed the petering out of the album's profile, reaching #7 on the *Billboard* charts and going gold as a physical single on January 5, 1977. It also went gold in Canada, where it peaked at #5. The shockingly easy-listening piano ballad spent a total of twenty-one weeks on *Billboard*. Of note, "Beth" was issued as an A-side in the United Kingdom, backed with "God of Thunder," almost a month before it appeared as a B-side to "Detroit Rock City," let alone A-side, perhaps telegraphing the switcheroo to come.

Concerning the album as a whole, *Destroyer* got to #11 on the *Billboard* charts, hanging around for fourteen weeks. It stalled at #22 in the United Kingdom (after entering at #37, and that's with a ton spent on promotion, mostly announcing the European tour). It lasted for seventy-eight weeks on Cash Box, peaking at #7 on week six. It got to #6 in both Australia and Canada and also marked the first time the band charted in New Zealand and Germany. It was certified gold in the United States on April 22, 1976, and platinum on November 11 of the same year, achieving double platinum on September 9, 2011.

Peter's famed "Beth" nightly spotlight often involved red roses.

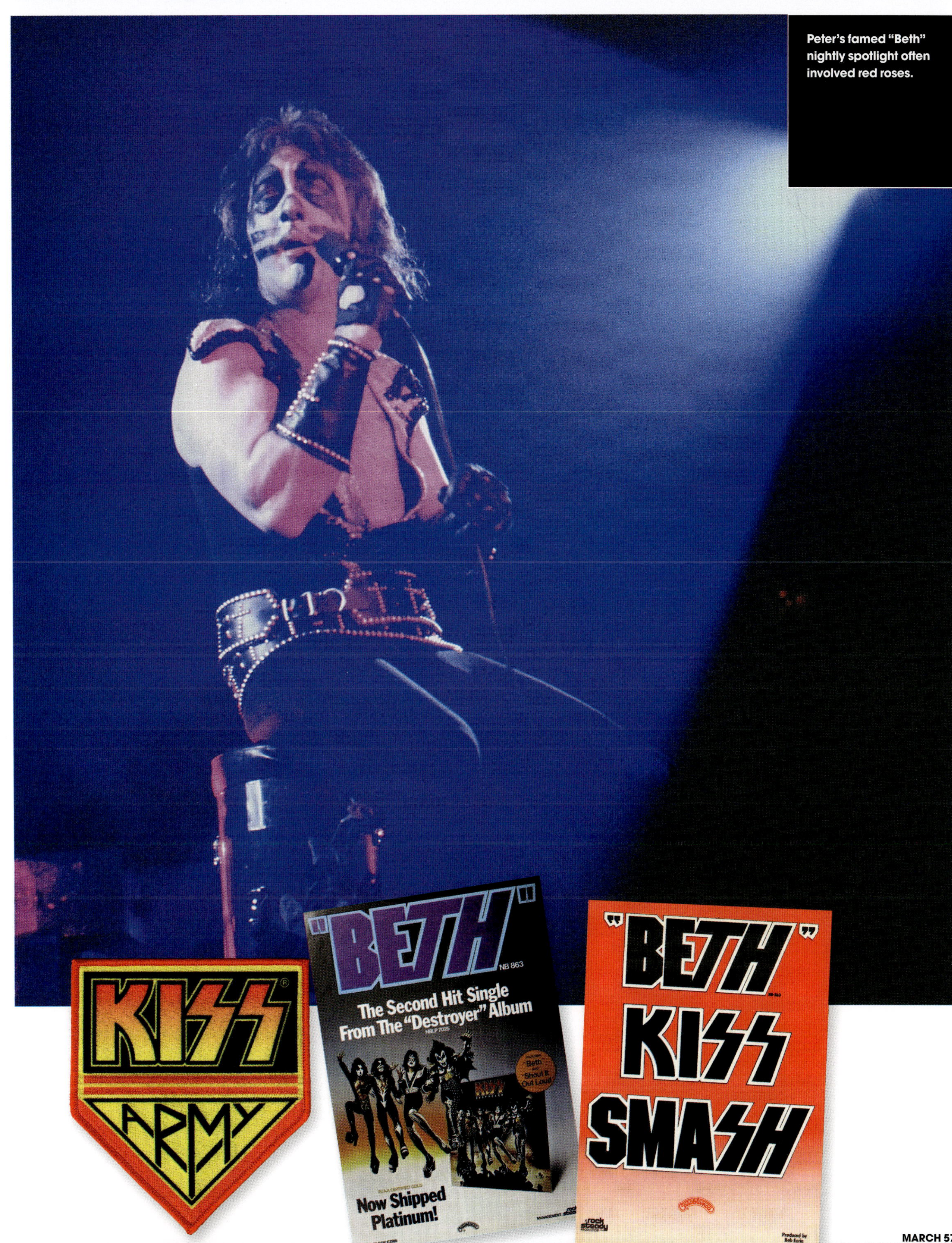

Following spreads: Gene packing a lunchbox and going to work at the Assembly Center, Tulsa, Oklahoma, March 8, 1976.

Publicity photo shot from 1976, courtesy of the legendary Fin Costello, creator of the *Alive!* cover image.

JANUARY

FEBRUARY

MARCH

APRIL

MAY

JUNE

JULY

AUGUST

SEPTEMBER

OCTOBER

NOVEMBER

DECEMBER

A nicely composed Fin Costello portrait shows off the band's new costumes. The image came from a whirlwind, multi-photographer session conducted April 9, two days before the official beginning of the *Destroyer* campaign in Fort Wayne, Indiana.

APRIL '76 TOUR DATES

April 11	**Allen County War Memorial Coliseum**	**Fort Wayne, IN**
April 13	**Memorial Auditorium**	**Utica, NY**
April 14	**Convention Center**	**Niagara Falls, NY**
April 16	**Bangor Auditorium**	**Bangor, ME**
April 18	**Moncton Coliseum**	**Moncton, NB**
April 19	**Halifax Forum**	**Halifax, NS**
April 21	**Forum Concert Bowl**	**Montreal, PQ**
April 22	**Civic Center**	**Ottawa, ON**
April 23	**Kitchener Auditorium**	**Kitchener, ON**
April 24	**London Arena**	**London, ON**
April 26	**Maple Leaf Gardens**	**Toronto, ON**
April 28	**Winnipeg Arena**	**Winnipeg, MB**

The band kicked off the month with rumors swirling about an impending comic book as well as the formation of their own film company. But soon, Paul, Gene, Ace, and Peter got in a photo shoot on April 9, before the impending *Spirit of '76* tour. This was conducted with Barry Levine, working primarily at Mothers Sound Stage, on East Fifth Street in New York. Levine told me, back in 2010: "I've always been known in my work to be more of a conceptualist, as opposed to just getting a band and shooting in front of a brick background or a white paper. I've always spent more time on either shooting a band or doing something more metaphorical. The two bands I always had fun with were Queen and Kiss, because they reveled in the theatrical. Queen had more focus on their music, but there was a certain theatrical glam aspect to Freddie (Mercury), the way Freddie presented himself. Whereas Kiss was balls-to-the-wall theatrical, whether you like their music or not. The first thing that motivated me, it gave me the opportunity to create sets that were more three-dimensional, as opposed to that one-dimensional perspective that people would see. Kiss is a business. Those guys go out and they perform as a business. They present a living, breathing, theatrical show, as you would see in Vegas or Broadway."

Maple Leaf Gardens, Toronto, Ontario, April 26. Support came from Hammersmith, a two-record Mercury act from Calgary, Alberta.

April 1976 begins with history in the making when Steve Jobs, Steve Wozniak, and Ronald Wayne found Apple Computer. A couple weeks later, Wayne sells back his 10 percent share for $800. Also on this day, surreal/expressionist artist Max Ernst dies at the age of eighty-four, and *Helter Skelter*, documenting the murder spree of the Charles Manson cult, debuts as a TV show produced by Lorimar Television. Also soon to be a cultural touchstone among young Kiss fans, *Wonder Woman*, starring Lynda Carter, becomes a proper episodic TV show this month, after two sort of pilot runs at it in 1975. Finally, *The Rocky Horror Picture Show*, a modest inspiration on Kiss, through the

This page and following: **These "chopper" photos also came from the April 9 session at Mother's Sound Stage in New York City. Gene's girlfriend at the time, Star Stowe, was included in some of the shots.**

filter of New York City and the New York Dolls, begins regular midnight showings.

On April 5, reclusive industrialist Howard Hughes dies at the age of seventy, and on the same day, at the movies, there's a hit baseball comedy called *The Bad News Bears*. Two days later, *All the President's Men*, about the Watergate scandal,

opens in theaters, becoming the sixth biggest movie of the year.

If you don't buy that there's any Kiss in Max Ernst, Charles Manson, *Wonder Woman*, and *Rocky Horror*, consider the Screamin' Eagle, the world's fastest and tallest roller coaster, which opens at Six Flags St. Louis on April 10. Two days later, Anne Rice sees the

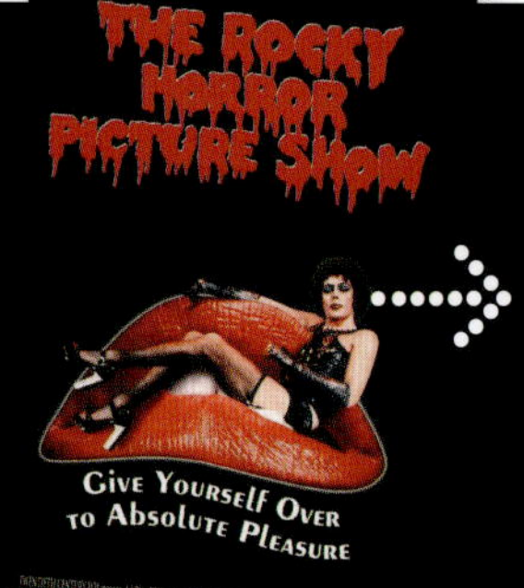

publication of *Interview with the Vampire*, and the day after that, the US Mint reintroduces the $2 bill, not produced since 1966. It's to commemorate the Bicentennial. On the front is Thomas Jefferson, but on the back, replacing an illustration of Jefferson's mansion, Monticello, is a depiction of the signing of the US Declaration of Independence. Gene, profoundly thankful for America taking in him and his mother, would approve. Coincidental with the explosive ascendance of the Kiss Army, on April 14, the Lion Country Safari near Mason, Ohio, suffers the escape of fifty baboons, all of which are rounded up and recaptured inside of a week.

Paul gives his hair some volume and shares a bit of product with the photographer in New York City.

IN MUSIC NEWS...

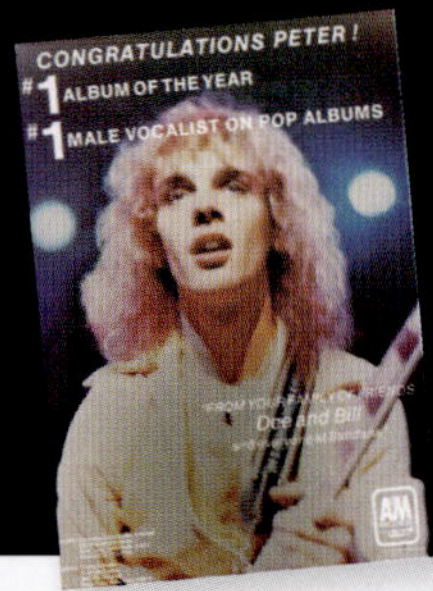

On April 8, Peter Frampton's *Frampton Comes Alive!* is certified platinum. The ex–Humble Pie guitarist is enjoying a career renaissance much like Mick Fleetwood and John McVie, who are commandeering a revitalized Fleetwood Mac. Also a big deal is Starland Vocal Band's "Afternoon Delight." Issued this month, the

song hits #1 on July 10, becoming ubiquitous on radio for the rest of the year, when it wasn't competing with "Convoy" from C.W. McCall, another one-hit wonder.

At the other end of the musical spectrum, on April 23, the Ramones issue their self-titled debut, which is considered the first punk rock album. Like Kiss, the band

In the end, Levine figures: "I'm proud of Kiss *Alive!* I worked with Kiss from '75 right up until they took their makeup off, and then I didn't really want to do it anymore. Then they were like any other band to me. When they put their makeup back on, they had me spend three days doing a whole studio shoot for them. It was fun."

Back to 1976, on April 10, it was announced in the press that *Alive!* had gone gold in Canada. Also on that day, *Destroyer* was issued in Japan, complete with new Obi strip design that would be in use until 1980. *Dressed to Kill* was the first Kiss album issued in Japan (July 25, 1975), followed by *Alive!* and now *Destroyer*, which finally ignited Kissmania in Japan, prompting the release of *Kiss* and *Hotter Than Hell*.

The band began touring duties at the Allen County War Memorial Coliseum in Fort Wayne, Indiana, on April 11, with Artful Dodger supporting. The band was still using its *Alive!* staging and costumes and only "Shout It Out Loud" in the set in terms of new songs, soon to be joined by "Flaming Youth" and "God of Thunder" and, by the end of the month, "Detroit Rock City."

The rest of the month consisted of a Canadian leg, beginning just up from Maine at the Moncton Coliseum, Moncton, New Brunswick on April 18. Notably, (a) the band played the Civic Center in Ottawa, Ontario, on April 22, the day *Destroyer* was certified by the RIAA as gold, and (b) in Ottawa, Gene set his hair on fire. The show also provided the first known footage of "God of Thunder" being performed—and in the *Alive!* costumes.

Preceding the third encore at the next show, at the Maple Leaf Gardens in Toronto on April 26 (using the concert bowl configuration), a dozen members of the Kiss Army were called upon to present Canadian gold and platinum awards to the band. After the show, venue owner Bill Ballard, promoter Donald "Donald K. Donald" Tarlton, and producer Ezrin convened with the band at a party put on by Quality Records. The last performance of the Canadian campaign took place on April 28 (the author's thirteenth birthday), at the Winnipeg Arena in Winnipeg, Manitoba. Supporting in Canada were Mercury Records (Canada) artists Hammersmith, good for two albums—and one of the first rock concerts ever seen by the author, at the local hockey arena in Nelson, British Columbia, back in the day.

To close out the month on April 27, Ace celebrated his twenty-fifth birthday, and then three days later, "Flaming Youth" was issued as a single.

But the press was still playing catch-up, with any and all column inches appreciated. The April 1976 issue of *Hit Parader* included an uncredited review of the previous year's *Alive!* spread, indicating that "the realization that these guys have learned to make noise like the two-record Kiss *Alive!* is heartening. Instead of taking the cheapshot and coasting along on the Frederick's-of-Hades duds they copped from Alice and the heavy metal sludge inherited from their forefathers, it seems they've really been making an effort to learn their trade. This isn't to suggest that Kiss succeed on any kind of originality level. They borrow musical phrases like Hitler borrowed countries, and we could play Where-did-that-lick-come-from? all night but who's counting. I'm just pleased that they've got enough respect for the form that feeds them that they've attempted to master its clichéd vernacular."

Later, the writer conjures some amusing comparatives, writing of the live rendition of "Strutter" that "the vocal has a redneck accent sauced over what was once Brooklynese, so it comes out sounding like the lead singer of Iron Butterfly pretending to be Jim Dandy Mangrum. It's better than a lot of Grand Funk, and even stands up pretty well against quality stuff like the Cooper repertoire, though admittedly minus the lyrical imagination."

members are downtown New Yorkers, with both bands having their separate cultural connections to the New York Dolls but not much overlap with each other, save for the fact they both have uniforms and easily digestible songs. As well, both draw connection and comparison to the Dictators and Blue Öyster Cult. In terms of shocking stage show, the Tubes were one of the few who could compete with Kiss. Fee Waybill and the boys issue their second album, *Young and Rich*, this month.

Also specifically on April 23, Jethro Tull issue *Too Old to Rock 'n' Roll: Too Young to Die!*, which, supporting an earlier point about prog waning, is the first 1970s album by the band not to certify. Also underscoring this narrative, Emerson, Lake & Palmer don't have an album in 1976—or 1975 or 1974—and King Crimson is long gone. Still on April 23, AC/DC play their first UK concert, at the Red Cow in London, and the Rolling Stones issue *Black and Blue*, which is certified gold three days later and platinum on June 23. If there's

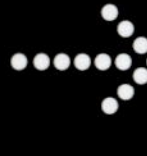

greater rock royalty than the Stones, it's the Beatles, who, the next day, are offered the princely sum of $3,000 by Lorne Michaels to reunite for an appearance on the hot hand of a comedy show for any Kiss fan of the day, *NBC's Saturday Night Live*. With Paul McCartney and John Lennon both in town at the time, they considered showing up.

On April 26, Parliament score a gold record with *Mothership Connection*, bringing additional success to the Casablanca label. Elton John issues a live album called *Here and There*, and Bruce Springsteen tries to get into Graceland to see Elvis by scaling the fence. He's caught by security guards, who escort him off the premises, telling him Elvis is out

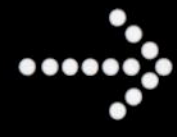

RAI Congrescentrum, Amsterdam, May 23. Supporting was Finch, a Dutch progressive rock act good for three albums between 1975 and 1977.

of town. Springsteen is another East Coast act who is a hot hand at the time, with his *Born to Run* having gone gold in October the previous year.

Besides the Frampton, Fleetwood Mac, and Kiss albums, two of the big sellers, all in the *Billboard* Top Ten this month, are Johnnie Taylor's *Eargasm*, Bad Company's *Run with the Pack*, Olivia Newton-John's *Come on Over*, Captain & Tenille's *Song of Joy*, Bob Dylan's *Desire*, Paul Simon's *Still Crazy after All These Years*, and two albums from the Eagles, the hits compilation and *One of These Nights*. Conclusion? For rock in the Top Ten, there's Peter Frampton and Bad Company—and that's it.

JANUARY
FEBRUARY
MARCH
APRIL
MAY '76
JUNE
JULY
AUGUST
SEPTEMBER
OCTOBER
NOVEMBER
DECEMBER

From a publicity photo session conducted on May 10 upon arrival in London.

May '76 Tour Dates

May 4	**River Trails Junior High**	**Mount Prospect, IL (M&M contest concert)**
May 13	**Free Trade Hall**	**Manchester, ENG**
May 14	**Odeon**	**Birmingham, ENG**
May 15	**Hammersmith Odeon**	**London, ENG**
May 16	**Hammersmith Odeon**	**London, ENG**
May 18	**Rosengarten**	**Mannheim, FRG**
May 19	**Philipshalle**	**Düsseldorf, FRG**
May 22	**Olympia**	**Paris, FRA**
May 23	**RAI Congrescentrum**	**Amsterdam, NLD**
May 24	**Stadthalle**	**Offenbach, FRG**
May 26	**Scandinavium**	**Gothenburg, SWE**
May 28	**Gröna Lund**	**Stockholm, SWE**
May 29	**Falkoner Teatret**	**Copenhagen, DEN**
May 30	**Olympen**	**Lund, SWE**

On May 1, Ace married Jeanette Trerotola, and Kiss performed at the happy couple's reception, which took place at the Americana Inn in Manhattan. Also on this day, "Shout It Out Loud" reached its peak on the *Billboard* charts at #31, and in that issue of the magazine, Nat Freedland interviewed Aucoin.

Writes Freedland, "Huge outdoor stadiums may not necessarily be the best venues for rock concerts by star attractions which could fill either a stadium or multiple dates at an arena. So says Bill Aucoin, whose Rock Steady management firm has guided Kiss through a phenomenal three-year club from nowhere to probably the hottest new rock record and concert group."

Explains Aucoin in the piece, "The new Kiss show starts out in June and will probably do 50 dates by the end of summer. I don't expect to play more than six or so stadiums. Let's face it, there is great media impact in filling a major market stadium with Kiss, a group that didn't even have a record out three years ago.

AMERICA FELL FOR HARD-ROCKING KISS

In 1973, an unknown opening act called KISS exploded onto the stage of New York's Academy of Music. At the end of the first number, the audience sat rigid and dumbfounded.

The group proceeded with the next number, "Fire House," along with the flames, the smoke, and the explosions that are an integral part of it. Gene Simmons' hair caught fire, but his concentration was so intense, he was completely unaware of the three-foot flames. Production manager, Sean Delaney, rushed on stage to smother the blaze with a coat. The audience was aghast. The featured act wanted KISS to get off the stage.

KISS has all of the extraordinary stage effects under control now, and the audiences, too! Fans are clamoring to the box offices, breaking attendance records in cities across the country.

The meteoric success of KISS is nowhere better seen than on the record charts. The first two albums, KISS and Hotter Than Hell, each sold over a quarter of a million copies. Dressed To Kill sold over 300,000. The fourth album, Alive! has soared to the top to the delight of KISS stars Gene Simmons, Peter Criss, Paul Stanley and Ace Frehley, as well as their manager, William M. Aucoin, and Casablanca Records President Neil Bogart. Alive!

CASABLANCA RECORDS • 8255 SUNSET BLVD. LOS ANGELES, CA 90046 • (213) 650-8300

This page and following spread: **Amsterdam, May 23, was the midpoint of the band's first European campaign, not entirely a cheery tour, given their disappointment at the reduced size of the venues. This show was before a crowd of about 1,400.**

IN WORLD NEWS...

On May 2, the Super Proton Synchrotron at CERN, straddling the border between France and Switzerland, fires up in search of re-creating the Big Bang (or something to that effect). Concerns crop up that if things go wrong, the Earth might be reduced to the size of a charred and ridiculously heavy basketball. In related news, six days later the Revolution roller coaster opens at Six Flags Magic Mountain—it's the first steel roller coaster with a vertical flip. Also related, on May 24, the supersonic Concorde is put into commercial use.

On May 16, the Montreal Canadiens win the Stanley Cup, defeating the Philadelphia Flyers. If you were a young male Kiss fan

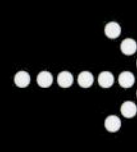

in 1976, or more pertinently if you were in my gang of buddies, you looked up to the brawling Broad Street Bullies Flyers teams of 1972 and 1973, along with the high-scoring Boston Bruins. And there was a link to the heroes of our story. The boys and I used to draw Gene, Paul, Peter, and Ace nearly as much as we'd draw goalies off our favorite hockey card poses—the connection is in the masks. Also in hockey news, on May 23, the Winnipeg Jets win the World Hockey Association championship. This was a fairly big deal of a league that was billed as a challenge to the NHL, which it lived up to for a few struggling years.

Over to football, there's only one NFL team that looked like Kiss, and that's the Oakland Raiders. They won Super Bowl XI on January 9, 1977, which is the culmination of the 1976 season. Plus, quarterback Kenny Stabler looked like a rock star. Otherwise, the Pittsburgh Steelers enjoyed a bit of a dynasty in the late 1970s—and we liked them, too, because they were tough. Speaking of tough, on May 24, a

late-career Muhammad Ali defeats Richard Dunn in Munich to win the heavyweight boxing title. This follows upon a great rivalry in the early 1970s with Joe Frazier that made many a young male—and Kiss fan, for they are one and the same—also a boxing fan. Kiss, on tour in Europe at the time, actually watch the Ali/Dunn fight on TV.

Over to television, on May 17, *The Mary Tyler Moore Show* cleans up at the Emmys—and yes, we were all fans of the show. Mary herself hosts the Emmys, along with John Denver, who is a huge multiplatinum star at the time, and, along with Barry Manilow, thought to be the polar opposite of Kiss, with both being the butt of whatever passed for memes

A publicity shot, also from the band's visit to Amsterdam. In addition to the Netherlands and UK dates, the inaugural European tour included shows in Germany, France, Sweden, and Denmark.

in 1976. Also in TV news, May 11 marks the last broadcast of *Marcus Welby, MD*, which also figured in jokes many cracked at the time. Over to film, *Taxi Driver* wins the Palme d'Or at the Cannes Film Festival on May 28. Less highbrow, on May 26, *Mother, Jugs & Speed* premieres in theaters. It stars Bill Cosby as Mother, Raquel Welch as Jugs, and Harvey Keitel as Speed. It does big business the following month, hitting #1 at the box office on June 24.

On a more serious note, the debate over the fate of coma patient Karen Ann Quinlan is constantly in the news. On May 22, her parents won the right to remove her from life support, although she miraculously continued to breathe on her own, living for another nine years. Kiss brethren, Starz, linked through manager Bill Aucoin, had a song on their first album about the tragic situation called "Pull the Plug."

IN MUSIC NEWS...

Come May 1976, there's the one that got away: Gene produces a demo for Van Halen, working at Village Recorders Studios in Los Angeles and Electric Lady in New York. Eventually Aucoin passes on the band, and the partnership fizzles. Also in the same part of the alphabet, UFO issue the strident and rocking *No Heavy Petting,* and Uriah Heep issue *High and Mighty,* which isn't strident, rocking, high, or mighty. Uriah Heep would support Kiss on multiple dates at the start of the *Rock and Roll Over* tour in December 1976 into 1977. Their glory years are now over, evidenced in the fact that Rush supported them in 1974, and then the bill switched in later years. Also this month,

But except for the charge of energy a giant audience might give the performers, I feel an indoor show is fairer to the ticket buyer."

Back to Freedland, "Aucoin makes the somewhat surprising point that an artist may well take more profits from two or three nights in an indoor arena than from playing one show before the same number of people in a stadium."

Says Aucoin, "It costs a lot more, proportionally, to rent a stadium for a concert than to rent an arena. Also, the best concert sound can be gotten indoors, and at a stadium most of the audience is too far away to really see the artists."

Winning the gig through a promotion put on by Mars Candy Co. and Chicago station WCFL, River Trails Junior High School hosted a Kiss concert on May 4, with 350 students in attendance. It's the last time the band used the *Alive!* costumes.

Next, the band was scooped up and sent to the United Kingdom, where preparations were made for the band's first European tour. A photo shoot was conducted at various locations around London (including Heathrow, Buckingham Palace, and Westminster Bridge) on May 10, followed by two days of rehearsal at Shepperton Film Studios, which will also produce *The Omen*, one of the hit films of 1976.

The first European Kiss concert took place at the Free Trade Hall in Manchester, United Kingdom, on May 13, followed by Birmingham and two nights at the Hammersmith Odeon in London, during which time, back home, *Destroyer* reached its peak position on the *Billboard* charts at #11. Supporting on all UK dates is Stray.

Back home, the May 13 issue of *Circus* put a *Destroyer* ad on the back cover, plus a small feature in the Back Pages section, topped with a picture of the band with Elton John, thriving at this time. Paul talks about how excited he is about visiting the United Kingdom and how it was the British bands that pushed the concept of image. Writer Peter Crescenti notes that Paul's a big fan of the Beatles, the Move, and the Yardbirds. Over in the Top 20 of this issue, *Alive!* takes the #1 spot with *Destroyer* nowhere, indicating how out-of-date these polls are. Robert Plant is on the cover of the issue, with the Rolling Stones, Queen, and Grand Funk enjoying large features. In terms of wide pop culture, there are articles on Charles Bronson and the Reverend Sun Myung Moon.

Back in Europe, the UK dates were followed by shows in Germany, France, the Netherlands, Sweden, and Denmark. On May 28, the band executed a photo shoot with their longtime collaborator Barry Levine, as well as Hans Hatwig, at the Skansen Open-Air Museum in Stockholm.

On this inaugural overseas campaign, the band learned some hard lessons about touring Europe, mainly about how small the venues are, which is a real problem for a band with an elaborate stage show. Also, as Paul lamented at the time, the band had to "prove ourselves all over again. We were back at square one—nobodies." The gross for the entire tour wound up to be $60,695.

On a brighter note, the May 29 issue of *Billboard* reported that "the Kiss Army fan club has grossed more than $40,000 from a notice on the inner sleeve of the Kiss *Destroyer* album released in March. Total membership in the fan club is over 5,000 since it was formed in February, reports Boutwell Enterprises, concert merchandisers and licensing agents for Kiss. Members get a quarterly newspaper, posters, photos and information about new Kiss merchandise coming up."

Sammy Hagar embarks on a solo career, issuing a debut called *Nine on a Ten Scale*.

May 1, 1976, represents one of a handful of first gig dates for Iron Maiden, who will support Kiss on the European *Unmasked* tour in late 1980. Maiden would absolutely represent stiff competition for Kiss all through the 1980s, the early 1990s, and indeed all the time after Bruce Dickinson rejoined the band in 1999. Much more visceral in terms of competition for Kiss—in fact, as direct as it gets—on May 3, Aerosmith issue their *Rocks* album, a masterpiece, and like *Destroyer*, the band's fourth. Also on this day, Canada's Max Webster issue their self-titled debut, and Wings begin

Gene kicks out the jams in Amsterdam amid a hectic schedule that had the band in France the day before and Germany the day after.

their *Wings over America* tour. It's the first time Paul McCartney has performed in the United States since August 29, 1966, when the Beatles played Candlestick Park, their final proper show.

On May 12, Keith Relf of Yardbirds fame dies, at the age of thirty-three, from electrocution in his basement. By the end of the year, Ace would suffer his own electrocution accident, but for now, two days later, AC/DC issue *High Voltage*. On May 17, Rainbow issue their second album, *Rising*, with cover art by Ken Kelly, who is on record that he did the *Rising* cover after he did the *Destroyer* cover. *Rising* poses the challenge that quality heavy rock from the United

Kingdom is still possible. Speaking of the British, the next day David Bowie completes his *Isolar 1* tour, in Paris, after sixty-five dates. The day after that, Keith Richards is involved in a car crash; he's found carrying and is subsequently arrested.

Meanwhile, Billy Joel issues his *Turnstiles* album, which goes platinum, and then on May 21,

Outside Buckingham Palace, London, May 10.

local Kiss rivals Blue Öyster Cult issue *Agents of Fortune*, with its smash hit "(Don't Fear) the Reaper." Meanwhile, Sweet, whose early Chapman/Chinn hits sound like Kiss songs, enjoy the height of their success in the United States when *Desolation Boulevard* certifies gold, on the strength of "Fox on the Run" and "Ballroom Blitz," either of which would have sounded fine on a Kiss album.

Finally, on May 31, the Who scoop up the record for the loudest concert ever, registering a noise level of 126 dB, which breaks the previous record set by Deep Purple. With it, they get called "the loudest band in the world," with Kiss having to settle for "the hottest band in the land."

JUNE '76

One of the most famous promo shots of the band, helping to make their 1976 a year for the ages.

JUNE '76 TOUR DATES

June 2	**Volkshaus**	**Zürich, SUI**
June 3	**Circus Krone**	**Munich, FRG**
June 4	**MTV Grundig Halle**	**Nüremberg-Fürth, FRG**
June 6	**Ontmoetingscentrum**	**Harelbeke, BEL**

Circus kicks off the month with some nice coverage on the band in their June 1 issue, although Mick Jagger and Keith Richards take the front cover. It's a six-page feature all about the new *Destroyer* album, with two of the pages taken up by full-page shots of Gene and Paul. Elsewhere, there are stories on Bad Company, Rainbow, and Robin Trower, as well as drug laws, CB radio, and the Fonz. The back cover of the issue gets the *Destroyer* ad now seen repeatedly.

Kiss's European tour continues into early June, with the band playing the Volkshaus in Zürich, Switzerland, followed by Circus Krone in Munich, Germany, at which time they were interviewed backstage, with the interview and a live airing of the band's performance of "Detroit Rock City" showing up on Bayern 3 TV on July 16. Next came Nüremberg/Fürth, Germany, and Harelbeke, Belgium, on June 6 to close out the tour, with about 500 fans in attendance at a venue that holds 1,500.

The June 3 issue of *Rolling Stone* features a review of *Destroyer* by John Milward, who begins, "There's no doubt that *Destroyer* is Kiss' best album yet or that Bob Ezrin, Alice Cooper's heavy-handed wizard of heavy-metal production who helped write seven of the nine tunes here, has made the difference. But despite Ezrin's superb production, Kiss still lacks that flash of creative madness that could have made their music interesting, or at least listenable."

The God of Thunder has blood on his hands.

A SPECIAL KISS ALBUM FOR THEIR SUMMER TOUR FEATURING CUTS FOR ALL FORMATS.

NOT FOR RESALE 33⅓ RPM FROM CASABLANCA RECORDS

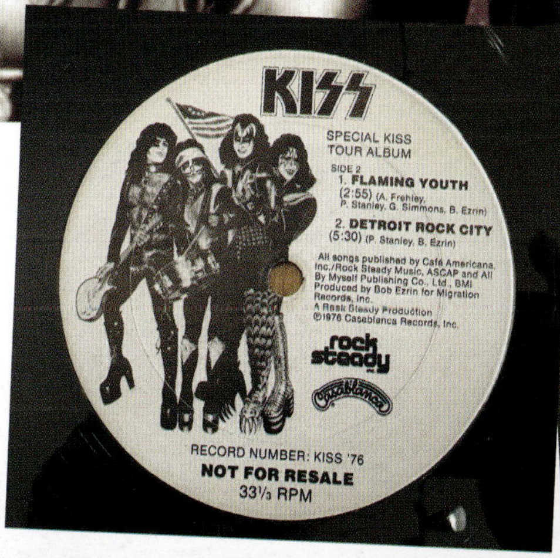

IN WORLD NEWS...

On June 2, the month kicks off with a really serious, high-technology bid to find the Loch Ness monster once and for all. It's a US expedition, and after six months, nothing is found. On June 6, famed billionaire Jean Paul Getty Sr. dies, the same day the Boston Celtics win the NBA championship.

In big pop culture news, June 14 marks the premiere of *The Gong Show*, created and emceed by Chuck Barris—it becomes must-see TV for kids in the Kiss demographic. In movie news, there's World War II epic *Midway* on June 18 and the dystopian *Logan's Run* on June 23. *Midway* in particular has cultural impact, given its use of Sensurround

He ends by saying, "Although constructed with professional aplomb, making use of a wide array of heavy-metal conventions, there's nothing new here. Even when an effective melody, such as the rabble-rousing 'Shout It Out Loud,' is presented, the lackluster performances dampen the effect. The vocals are undistinguished and emotionally empty; the lyrics—about partying and the rock scene, with plenty of campy S&M allusions—trite. Worse yet, there's not a memorable guitar solo on the album."

The cover of this issue features an illustration of Jimmy Carter, linked to a feature written by Hunter S. Thompson. Neither of the other two stories featured on the cover are about music. Among ads for stereo equipment, cigarettes, cars, and movies, there's the iconic ad for Aerosmith's *Rocks*, featuring the front cover in white rather than black. Also advertised are records by Ian Hunter, Camel, the Charlie Daniels Band, John McLaughlin, the Crusaders, Firefall, Mahogany Rush, Dr. Hook, Greg Kihn, Fools Gold, and Three Dog Night. There is no ad for *Destroyer*. Bands written up include the Beach Boys, Led Zeppelin, Eric Clapton, and Donovan. Thin Lizzy's *Jailbreak* is reviewed in the same issue.

Kiss return to America and set about preparing for the *Destroyer* tour proper, deemed *The Spirit of '76* tour. The locale is Hanger E, at Stewart International Airport in Newburgh, New York, with the press invited to check it out. Plans call for a private jet, a TV crew, and a forty-person road crew, along with two tour busses and seven trucks to carry the show. The operation begins on June 16 and ends with a filmed dress rehearsal on June 27, with the band performing the likes of "Detroit Rock City," "King of the Night Time World," "Let Me Go, Rock 'n' Roll," and more. At this point they are using the new staging, designed by Mark Ravitz for Jules Fisher Associates. They've also got the new costumes, designed by Larry LeGaspi, which cost the band $4,775.

Meanwhile, on June 19, "Flaming Youth" reaches its *Billboard* peak at #74, and on June 24, Kiss execute the legendary photo shoot atop the Empire State Building, conducted by

Ace with one of his trusty and traditional sunburst Les Pauls.

technology, making the theater shake like the end of "Black Diamond" on Kiss *Alive!* On June 25, *The Omen* opens in theaters, quickly becoming the biggest hit horror movie since *The Exorcist*.

On June 23, the United Kingdom is ravaged by a heat wave and drought that lasts all summer. Two days later, having just dealt with an assassination attempt that killed two members of his entourage, Uganda's president, Idi Amin, declares himself president for life. In office from 1971 to 1979, "Big Daddy" is everybody's favorite dictator of the 1970s, or at least the butt of many jokes—again, in modern-day parlance, a pop culture meme.

This page: **Paul and Gene corrupt one of New York's finest (top) and the classic Empire State Building shoot (below).**

Barry Levine. The session includes shots on the streets of New York City and in Central Park. At the top of the skyscraper, the band was pretty freaked out, but Ace and Peter were also boozed up on champagne, which had alarmed Gene, who didn't want to lose any band members off the side of the building.

On June 26, Toronto, Ontario, scoops up some bragging rights when the CN Tower opens to the public. It reigns as the world's tallest freestanding structure until usurped by the Burj Khalifa skyscraper in Dubai in 2009. In US Bicentennial news, also on June 26, the first of a fleet of "tall ships" arrives (from Argentina) in Newport, Rhode Island, in preparation for an event planned for New York's harbor on July 4. Also on this day, beloved boxer Muhammad Ali is still very much in our lives, as he fights Japanese wrestler Antonio Inoki in a bout called the War of the Worlds. Back to Bicentennial preparations, the biggest American flag to date gets wrecked by the wind as it's displayed hung from the Verrazzano-Narrows Bridge in New York City. It's of little consequence, though, because it will be Barry Levine and Kiss that will stitch together the event's lasting images.

IN MUSIC NEWS...

On June 3, Queen's high-concept "Bohemian Rhapsody" certifies gold as a single, with Freddie Mercury, Brian May, John Deacon, and Roger Taylor packing more ideas into one song than producer Ezrin could stuff into *Destroyer*. In other royal news, the night before the wedding of King Carl XVI Gustaf of Sweden to Silvia Sommerlath, ABBA go on

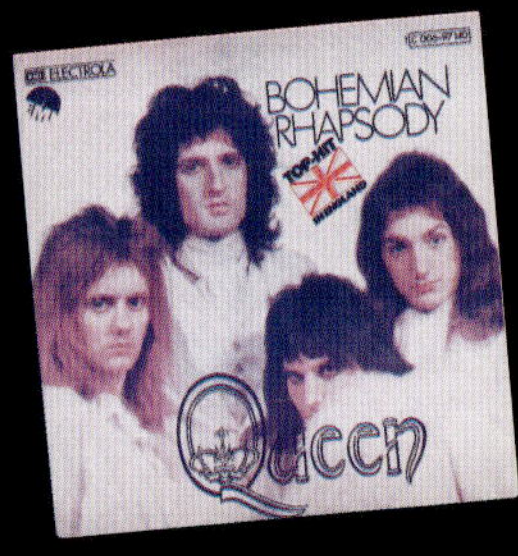

Swedish TV and perform "Dancing Queen" for the first time.

Also this month, Casablanca recording artists Angel issue their second album, *Helluva Band*. It's got a "Dr. Ice" on it, and Kiss will soon be "Calling Dr. Love." It's also got an original on it called "Anyway You Want It," whereas Kiss will be covering a Dave Clark Five song

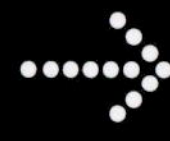

Kiss puts their mark on their hometown, The City That Never Sleeps.

called that on their *Alive II* album the following year. Dressed all in white, Angel are marketed as the antithesis to Kiss. For the next couple of years, the band is going to be promoted heavily.

Explains Casablanca's Larry Harris, "We tried to get Kiss to take Angel on tour with them, because Gene is the person who called us to tell us about Angel to start with. So, we thought it would be a no-brainer. But then we were in a contractual dispute with Kiss at the time that Angel's first album was coming out. They refused to take any of our bands with them, and that's how Rush got on their first tour with Kiss, which helped break Rush." Angel's third album, 1977's *As It Is in Heaven*, will be produced by Eddie Kramer, who also mans the board for *Alive!*, *Rock and Roll Over*, and *Love Gun*. Mixing is right-hand man Corky Stasiak, also a vital part of the Kiss story. Perhaps logically, it's this third Angel album that sounds the most like a Kiss album. Kramer is also at the helm for Mott's *Shouting and Pointing* record, issued on June 7.

Mott is Mott the Hoople without Ian Hunter.

On June 21, New Jersey act Starz enjoy the release of their self-titled debut on Capitol. Managed by Bill Aucoin, they are seen as an up-and-coming band that might emerge as rivals to Kiss—they've even got their own Motor City song, called "Detroit Girls," plus a pointy logo and an

embossed album cover, just like *Dressed to Kill*. "Starz I was directly involved with," affirms Aucoin. "Michael Lee Smith, I always thought, was one of the best writers going. He is just a phenomenal writer, and if you listen to those albums that Starz did, they are way ahead of their time. In fact, I can't believe that other artists haven't

A truly disturbing shot of Gene from the summer of '76.

copied more of those songs. Some of those songs are absolutely brilliant. And Michael was a great frontman as well. I loved that group, and unfortunately it fell apart."

Four days after the Starz album, Alice Cooper issues *Alice Cooper Goes to Hell*, with the brunt of the album written by Cooper, Ezrin, and Dick Wagner, who, as discussed, were guests on *Destroyer*. The album includes "I Never Cry," which feels like a follow-up to "Beth." The band's tour for the album, however, is canceled after Cooper collapses due to substance abuse issues, on June 10. Speaking of boozing, also on this day, Uriah Heep play their last show with David Byron.

In summary, it's an interesting month in that three acts very much regularly compared to Kiss, or in the same conversations with Kiss, all released albums. One can frame Alice Cooper as the foundational or precursor band and can frame both Angel and Starz as proposed upstart bands doing somewhat the same thing—baby Kiss bands, as it were.

JANUARY
FEBRUARY
MARCH
APRIL
MAY
JUNE
JULY
AUGUST
SEPTEMBER
OCTOBER
NOVEMBER
DECEMBER

'76

Comic book hero status achieved: Toledo Sports Arena, Toledo, Ohio, July 31.

JULY '76 TOUR DATES

July 3	The Scope	Norfolk, VA
July 6	Carolina Coliseum	Columbia, SC
July 8	Coliseum	Richmond, VA
July 10	Roosevelt Stadium	Jersey City, NJ
July 11	Cape Cod Coliseum	South Yarmouth, MA
July 13	Civic Center	Baltimore, MD
July 15	Civic Coliseum	Knoxville, TN
July 17	Civic Center	Charleston, WV
July 19	Freedom Hall Civic Center	Johnson City, TN
July 21	Municipal Auditorium	Nashville, TN
July 23	Rickwood Stadium	Birmingham, AL
July 26	Municipal Auditorium	Kansas City, MO
July 28	Kiel Auditorium	St. Louis, MO
July 29	Kiel Auditorium	St. Louis, MO
July 31	Sports Arena	Toledo, OH

On July 3, at the Scope in Norfolk, Virginia, Kiss kicked off a full-scale US tour in support of *Destroyer*, playing most of the new album, with a conspicuous absence being "Beth." For a stage set, the band presented a loose interpretation of the album cover, a ruined cityscape. Next up were Columbia, South Carolina; Richmond, Virginia; and Jersey City, New Jersey, where the J. Geils Band and Bob Seger provided strong support at the outdoor event (Seger and his Silver Bullet Band were recurring support throughout the tour). Press was invited from around the county, with Aucoin creating a "Little Italy" backstage.

The July 10 edition of industry magazine *Record World* featured Barry Levine's Bicentennial-themed shot of Kiss on the cover. *Alive!* was in their chart at #41, with *Destroyer* at #67. *Fleetwood Mac* is #1, with an ad touting double-platinum success. The same Kiss shot was used on the cover of the July issue of *Creem*, which also included an experimental sort of future-themed story on the band plus a *Destroyer* album review.

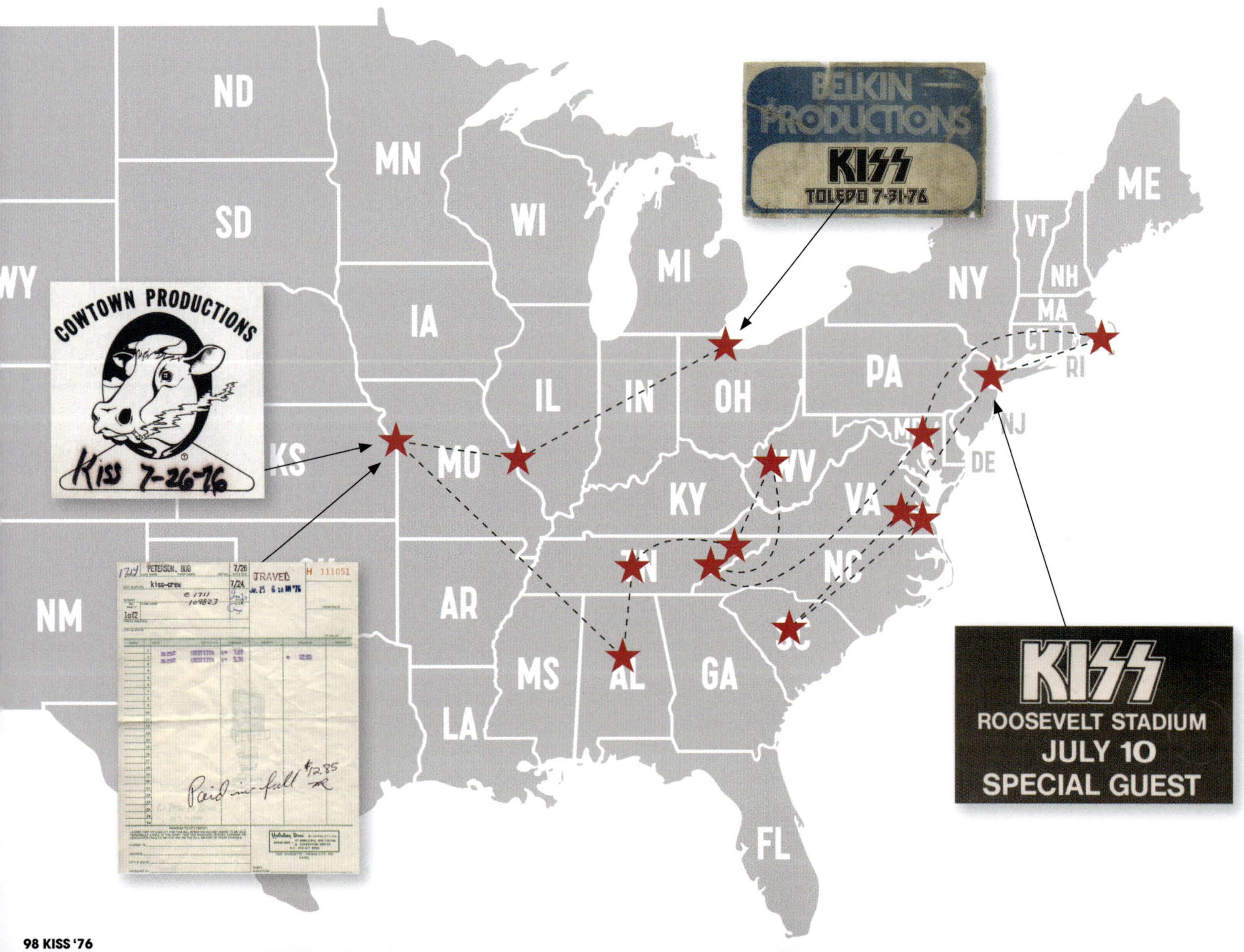

You see, he plays so fast that the guitar catches . . . oh, never mind. Municipal Auditorium, Kansas City, Missouri, July 26.

IN WORLD NEWS...

July 1976 kicks off with a couple of cultural icons winning at Wimbledon (July 2 and 3), namely Chris Evert and Björn Borg, the first appreciated by Kiss fans because of hormones and the second because he looked like a hippie.

Then it's time for America's Bicentennial celebrations, commemorating the break from Britain through the Declaration of Independence in 1776. Saying something about the strength of the industry, rock music delivered at a pile of outdoor festivals turns out to be a vehicle for the milestone event. Performing for big crowds across the country are the Eagles, Fleetwood Mac, ZZ Top, Lynyrd Skynyrd, and even Elvis Presley.

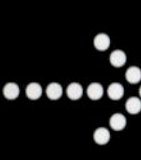

The July 6 issue of *Circus* covered Kiss as well, with a one-page article about their new private jet. They also appeared in the Back Pages section, with a story about the proposed comic book. In their Top 20, *Destroyer* was #1 and *Alive!* was #4. The July 22 issue included a two-page interview with Ace, and in the Top 20, *Destroyer* and *Alive!* took the top two slots. The ad on the back cover was for Angel's *Helluva Band* album, with the label heavily promoting the band, in search of a repeat phenomenon. In the wider pop culture realm, there was a feature on a show that was a hit with Kiss fans, schoolroom comedy *Welcome Back, Kotter*. Jeff Beck got the front cover, with major features on Nazareth, Blue Öyster Cult, and the Rolling Stones.

Remarks Gene, in the major *Record World* piece, written by David McGee, "Everybody was kind of talking about the death of exciting stage presentation. All the exciting things in rock 'n' roll had stopped. And here we were, a new band that was trying to take the next step beyond those great show bands that we watched when we were younger. So we tried to keep our music really straight ahead rock 'n' roll, no holds barred. And we gave the audience a show."

Asked by McGee about success, Paul adds, "It's great. We can spend more time now making better records, making better music. We have more opportunity to do things our way. We can see things through and make everything we want reality." Reflects Peter, "It's a big change for me, a punk kid from Brooklyn making it. I've been eating, drinking, sleeping Kiss for three years. Now Gene, this is his whole life, and Paul's too. Ace is Ace. First of all for me is my lady. I love Lydia; I've been with her for ten years. Gene's into money. I'm not. I'm into trying to get close to people, trying to get out of my paranoia, trying to share my fame with my wife."

"Kiss is right on time," vows producer Bob Ezrin. "And ready to cross the line between being a regional phenomenon and becoming a national phenomenon."

Dates at South Yarmouth, Massachusetts, and Baltimore, Maryland, were followed by

This page and following: **At the infamous gig on July 26 in Kansas City, Missouri, a concertgoer apparently turned on a firehose, flooding the main-level concourse outside the hall. Artful Dodger and Felix Pappalardi opened.**

The all-pervasive Elton John gets in on the act, even though he's British. A few days later, as the din dies down, disgraced former president Richard Nixon is disbarred from ever practicing law again.

In movie news, coast-to-coast road race comedy and David Carradine vehicle *Cannonball* is a big deal, hitting theaters July 6, to be followed by *The Gumball Rally* in August, essentially on the same Kiss fan-friendly topic. On the small screen, on July 12, *Family Feud* debuts, with popular droll host Richard Dawson, joining *The Price Is Right* with Bob Barker as top game shows of the era.

Back to the world of sports, the major story of the day is the staging of the 1976 Summer Olympics, in Montreal, Quebec, resulting in a renaissance for the city and a general flush of Canadian pride. The Games run from July 17 to August 1, and in the headlines is 14-year-old Romanian gymnast Nadia Comăneci, who, on July 18, scored a 10.00 for her uneven parallel bars routine, the first-ever perfect score in gymnastics. Another

star of the games is gold medalist Bruce Jenner, famed these days for transitioning into Caitlyn Jenner. Over to Major League Baseball, on July 20, home run record holder Hank Aaron hits his final dinger, preceding his retirement at the end of the 1976 campaign.

On July 21, the Viking 1 lander takes its first color photographs

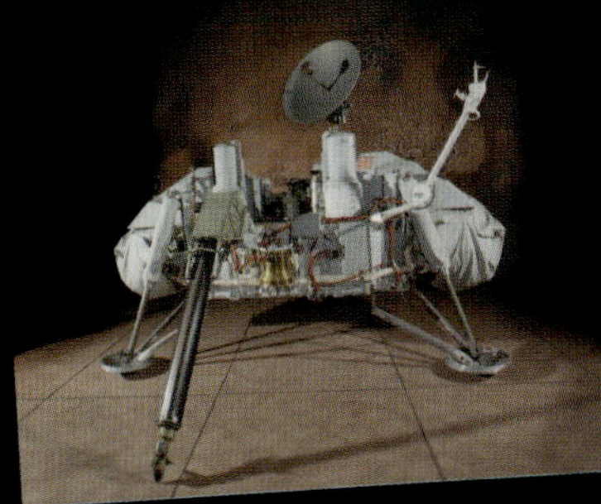

of Mars, showing the surface as reddish-colored and the sky as blue, which was not known at the time. On July 29, New York City serial killer David "Son of Sam" Berkowitz claims his first victim. Compounding the effect of Robert De Niro's fierce performance in *Taxi Driver*, along with crumbling infrastructure, the protracted crime

Robert Alford's inspiring photo from the Toledo Sports Arena on July 31 offers a unique vantage point portraying band and fan as one.

spree further tarnishes Kiss's hometown as violent and squalid. In fact, just the previous October, the city appealed to the federal government for bailout funds and was flatly rebuffed by President Gerald Ford. The *New York Daily News* ran the headline "FORD TO CITY: DROP DEAD," and although he never said that, it's long since been stuck into cultural lore that he had. As for Son of Sam, punk legends the Dead Boys wrote a song called that, and there were also songs about the scary New York City subway system from Starz and Blue Öyster Cult, two of our favorite Kiss-adjacent bands.

IN MUSIC NEWS . . .

On July 3, as part of the Bicentennial celebrations, the Beach Boys play Anaheim Stadium, marking the return of Brian Wilson after twelve years away. They co-headline with America. It's fitting given that the Beach Boys are the quintessential American band, along with Lynyrd Skynyrd, ZZ Top, and, to some extent, Kiss,

Another of Alford's imaginative Toledo vantage points shows Gene breathing fire, which didn't always go according to plan.

a swing through mid-South cities, with UFO jumping onto the bill at the last minute in Nashville, Tennessee, on July 21. Also on this day, Casablanca Records issued a three-LP Kiss package called *The Originals* (see feature) in Canada and the United States. The only other market to get *The Originals* was Japan.

Back to the tour, Kansas City was added to the bill, with the show on July 26 featuring Artful Dodger and Felix Pappalardi as openers. Two days later, on July 28, "Detroit Rock City" was issued as a single. The final July date, at Toledo, Ohio, saw Starz opening the show.

As Larry Harris from Casablanca explained to the author, the US Midwest constituted Kiss's bread and butter: "Absolutely; there's no doubt. Detroit broke Kiss. St. Louis and Detroit, really. Actually, Kiss were helped a great deal by Canadian stations at the time. Rosalie Tremblay, who ran CKLW in Windsor, Ontario, was the person who chose to go with the 'Beth' single. It was her choice what single they were going to go with. Actually, we didn't even want that single out. But St. Louis was big, too. Nobody would let Kiss open up for them after a while because it was too hard to follow. So, we had to throw in a great deal of money to make sure they were headliners in every market, even if they were never there before. Which we did. We bought tons of airtime and newspaper ads, everything. Plus, there were other factors happening. They had *Creem* magazine out of Detroit, which was pretty influential at the time. A lot of the headbanging, rock 'n' roll stations were in the Midwest. Cleveland is another example of that." While loving the flyover states, Harris wasn't dismissive of the coasts either. "Oh, the coasts got along with hard rock, but I think you have to prove yourself more. We did okay in LA; Kiss played the Forum many times. New York, we did okay; we did okay in Florida. There were pockets we didn't do well. Boston wasn't good for Kiss for a long time. San Francisco was a problem, but San Francisco always had this, 'We're San Francisco and we're cooler than everybody else' attitude, especially when Bill Graham was running the show there."

who swell with patriotism at this time. But it's Aerosmith who are coined "America's greatest rock 'n' roll band," and on July 9, *Rocks* is certified platinum, having reached gold quickly upon release in May.

Another shooting star of a patriot at the time, Ted Nugent, is finally seeing some success after a long obscure career, when his self-titled album from 1975 certifies gold on July 26. Bottom line, it's Kiss, Aerosmith, and Uncle Ted (aka Deadly Tedly, the Tedinator, the Whackmaster) who rule the latter half of decade, at least in the hearts and minds of young metalheads of a certain vintage. To be sure, there would be other important US bands (along with a few from the United Kingdom, Canada, and Australia), but there's a similarity of sound and career trajectory between these three that puts them in the same conversations over and over again.

Still tentatively in the conversation but fading fast (and really bigger a couple years earlier), Canada's Bachman-Turner Overdrive issue *Best of B.T.O. (So*

A fit Frehley pauses for some hydration at a backstage fountain.

Far), which goes platinum in the United States. It would be the last RIAA-certifying album for the band, after an impressive run of five golds in a row, reaching back to the band's 1973 debut. In essence, as Kiss struggled through to the end of 1975, BTO was kind of a big deal, making similar music. Perhaps symbolizing this late-arriving

ascendance of American hard rock acts, Deep Purple throws in the towel on July 19, putting an end to the band's experiment with hard funk, hard drugs, and Tommy Bolin. On a lighter note, the following week, Wings issue a new single, "Let 'Em In," which reaches #3 in the United Kingdom, Canada, and the United States. One can't lose

Ace and Paul partake of some six-string give and take at Toledo Sports Arena, July 31.

sight of the fact that pop is still the dominant force on the charts, despite many of us having blinders on and seeing only all things hot and heavy. At least that's the way things were back in the 1970s. Also, in Beatles news, John Lennon gets his green card, becoming a permanent resident alien of the United States.

THE ORIGINALS

If assembling two studio albums in 1976 wasn't enough, Kiss also repackaged their first three albums, issued on July 21 under the lofty title *The Originals*. Also lofty was the inclusion of a sixteen-page career retrospective booklet, along with a Kiss Army sticker and a set of six trading cards, even if the front cover lacked imagination, featuring the debut album photo behind a mushroom cloud. Then there was the fact that the band name and title were represented in simple drop-out white text, and the aesthetic was marred by hype text that read "The Albums That Touched Off a Rock & Roll Explosion, *Kiss, Hotter than Hell, Dressed to Kill*."

Inside the country-of-origin US *Originals*, there's a pouch on the left side of the gatefold and another on the right that holds the three albums, housed in paper reproduction sleeves of the original covers. The labels are Casablanca tan. Canada got a standard gatefold, with plain green labels for the first album, yellow for the second, and red for the third, all with the text in black. A variant had the first album with a blue label. Plus, there was even more descriptive text on the cover, outlining the contents, including a "giant" Kiss Army sticker. Japan stuck close to the plot but added lyric sheets plus, of course, requisite Obi strip, with Casablanca/Victor issuing the album on March 25, 1977. As a nice touch, exactly a year later, the label in Japan issued a package called *The Originals II*, which gave the fans *Destroyer, Rock and Roll Over*, and *Love Gun*. This would not be replicated in other territories.

In the United States, the first issue of *The Originals* was touted as a limited-edition release, but after quickly selling out, Casablanca printed up more, adding the missive Second Printing to the cover. With the new printing, the album sleeve reproductions were now printed on coated stock as opposed to the matte finish of the original.

The eight-track longbox (10½" × 4" (26.7 × 10.2 cm)) features three of the cards, with perforations all around, on one side and three on the other, with the booklet neatly folded in half and inserted. Oddly, *The Originals* was not issued on cassette, although Japan put it out on reel-to-reel.

As for the booklet, it's tastefully sepia-toned throughout, with rare shots and an essay in large type by Richard Robinson, who provides the broad strokes of the band's history from 1972 to 1975, in plain language that seems deliberately attuned for a young audience. People hear about The Great Kiss Off and the band's escapades in Cadillac, Michigan, and they see early tour posters and passes. I recall as a kid oohing and aahing over the first photo, on page three, in large part because it says, "This rare picture is the first publicity photo ever released by Kiss. Note the hand-lettered Kiss logo in the background and the low-budget attire." Of course now, decades later, there's the internet. Plus, Kiss has explained themselves and been explained by others uncommonly exhaustively, and as a result, there are many intimate, archival shots like this around.

The backs of the "six wallet-size full-color Kiss rock superstar cards" provide more band factoids in the breezy, fawning manner of the Robinson essay, and it's nice to see on the back of the Kiss Army one robust acknowledgment of Bill Starkey, who started the fan club back in Terre Haute, Indiana.

Exploring the music enclosed, one would suppose the kid who'd only heard *Destroyer* and/or *Alive!* wasn't going to be exactly shocked, if maybe a little underwhelmed. The third album, *Dressed to Kill* sounds neat and competent, conservatively recorded but good enough, but the first two albums might sound a little brash and eccentric, if also pleasing to a headbanging ear, in the main.

Richie Wise, coproducer of the first two albums with Kenny Kerner, recalled of those days, "Bill Aucoin was great guy. Loved him. He had a partner too. Did a lot of the staging in the early days. They were really good. There was Joyce (Biawitz), who ended up marrying (Neil) Bogart. Yeah, there was some friction there, somewhere along the line. But I never paid too much attention to that stuff. I was just the music guy; to me it was all about the music. I try to stay away from the politics of the thing. I didn't understand that there are politics involved!"

Concerning one of the key tracks on the self-titled debut and indeed *The Originals*, Ace told the author, "'Deuce' has an interesting history. It was one of the first Kiss songs I ever heard, when I auditioned for Kiss. I was the last person to join the band. Paul, Gene, and Peter performed it for me when I was auditioning, and they said, 'Here's the song,' and I played a guitar solo to it and two weeks later they hired me. And to this day, it's still one of my favorite Kiss songs. You know, the songs that sound hard are probably the easiest ones for me to play (*laughs*). Sometimes the slower ones, people think that when something is really fast it's quite hard. But that's not the case. Sometimes it's the slower ones that you really have to focus on."

Aucoin recalled the fragile circumstances that nonetheless resulted in these three albums: "One of the key things that most people don't know about Kiss is that their career could have ended twice, actually three times. One was when Warner Bros. told Neil Bogart . . . Warner Bros. were the ones who put up the money to start Casablanca Records, and they told him that they really didn't want to see him sign a band with makeup. And Neil called me one night and asked me whether or not I would go to the band and see if they would take off their makeup. And I said, 'I don't think that is ever going to happen.' Anyway, I told the band, and of course it was no. So, Neil had to make a decision on what to do based on letting the band go or not or whatever, and he decided to fight for it. That was the first time it could have been a little shaky.

"The second time is when Casablanca, still at Warner Bros., Neil was still there, and Neil was a great schmoozer, and one of his friends on the inside had passed him a memo sent down by the powers that be that said not to work the Kiss album, that Neil would come up with some better product and just to let the Kiss album die. That was the first Kiss album. So, that could have been the end of their career then. And Neil decided that he was deeply offended by this and left Warners, made a deal with them to pay back the money they had already put in over a period of time, mortgaged his house, and went to independent distributors to come up with the rest of the money to keep the company going and to put out the Kiss album. Very few people today would have put their company in jeopardy over one group. So, that could have been the end of them the second time.

"When we finally went out on tour, the first night, which was at the Academy of Music in New York, which became the Palladium years after. It's the first night Gene threw some flash paper. He was supposed to go to the candelabra and light the flash paper and throw it up in the air. It was supposed to come out of his hands. And when he did it, he was so nervous he threw it into the audience and burned a kid's face. The truth of the matter is that could have been the end as well because that kid could have sued Kiss, could have sued the record label—that would have been it. So, there were three times right at the beginning in the first six months that they could have been over. So, they made it through the three tests, and everything else is history."

Concerning the productions of the first three albums—logically, fans get heated when debating *Hotter Than Hell* and its turgid, gutted song—Aucoin is noncommittal. He reflected: "I don't know if any of them were bad. Kiss were never a great musical group per se. I think they were great rock-and-rollers and they had a feeling for that. Kenny Kerner and Richie Wise did the first couple of albums. They came from a rock 'n' roll background, and they understood the craziness. It was a great album to begin with, for Kiss. By the time we got to the third album, Casablanca was in really bad shape financially. And Neil said to me, 'Look, we can't afford to hire a producer; I'll produce the third album.' So, *Dressed to Kill* was produced by Neil, and the guys, basically. All of them sort of threw their hat into the ring because there wasn't any money to hire anybody.

"Then we went to the live album pretty much because of the same thing. If we're going to keep going here, I'm not sure we can go into the studio. Why don't we record a live album? And of course by that time we had a really good following on the road, and we were really getting a response, and the live album made the most sense. To come up with more songs and to do a studio album, I mean, there were a lot of reasons why it wasn't going to happen. But really the best reason was that the band had been out on the road and they didn't have the songs ready. And number two, the real response to Kiss wasn't on the radio. The albums were selling more and more, but we really didn't have the breakthrough on that side. But we were having a breakthrough with the live concerts. So, we did the concerts and hired Eddie Kramer, who was a terrific engineer and certainly captured Kiss well with that first live album. It really was exactly where the group was at at that time. And of course that was the big breakthrough."

And now with *The Originals*, the fans had a convenient way to catch up on all of the first three albums, and maybe even learn a few things with a little light reading, before catching their breath and seeing what their comic superheroes might do next.

Casablanca head Neil Bogart, in conversation with *Billboard*'s John Sippel, explained: "*The Originals* by Kiss entered *Billboard*'s Top LP & Tape chart at #91 with a star this week. We therefore should have little or no returns. That rarely happens with even the hottest artists. And look at the money dealers, racks, and our distributors save in not having to make returns. It's a step in the right profit direction for the entire industry. We definitely won't make more because short additional runs of the special inner sleeves, outer album jackets, and collateral materials would quickly erode that important profit. It hasn't hurt the sale of their latest two albums. In fact, it's helped the new albums. And selling 250,000 of each of the first three albums has put them all within striking distance of being certified gold."

With the profits culled from the set, Bogart says, "We were able to put $200,000 in TV time buys through the Howard Marks Agency, New York, from our profits to support their current touring. We also did some radio and print advertising."

The Originals got to #40 on the *Cashbox* charts, staying on the grid for sixteen weeks. It peaked at #36 on *Billboard*, with a seventeen-week run in the charts. Canada's RPM chart had it at #54. *The Originals* has never been issued on CD.

JANUARY
FEBRUARY
MARCH
APRIL
MAY
JUNE
JULY
AUGUST
SEPTEMBER
OCTOBER
NOVEMBER
DECEMBER

'76

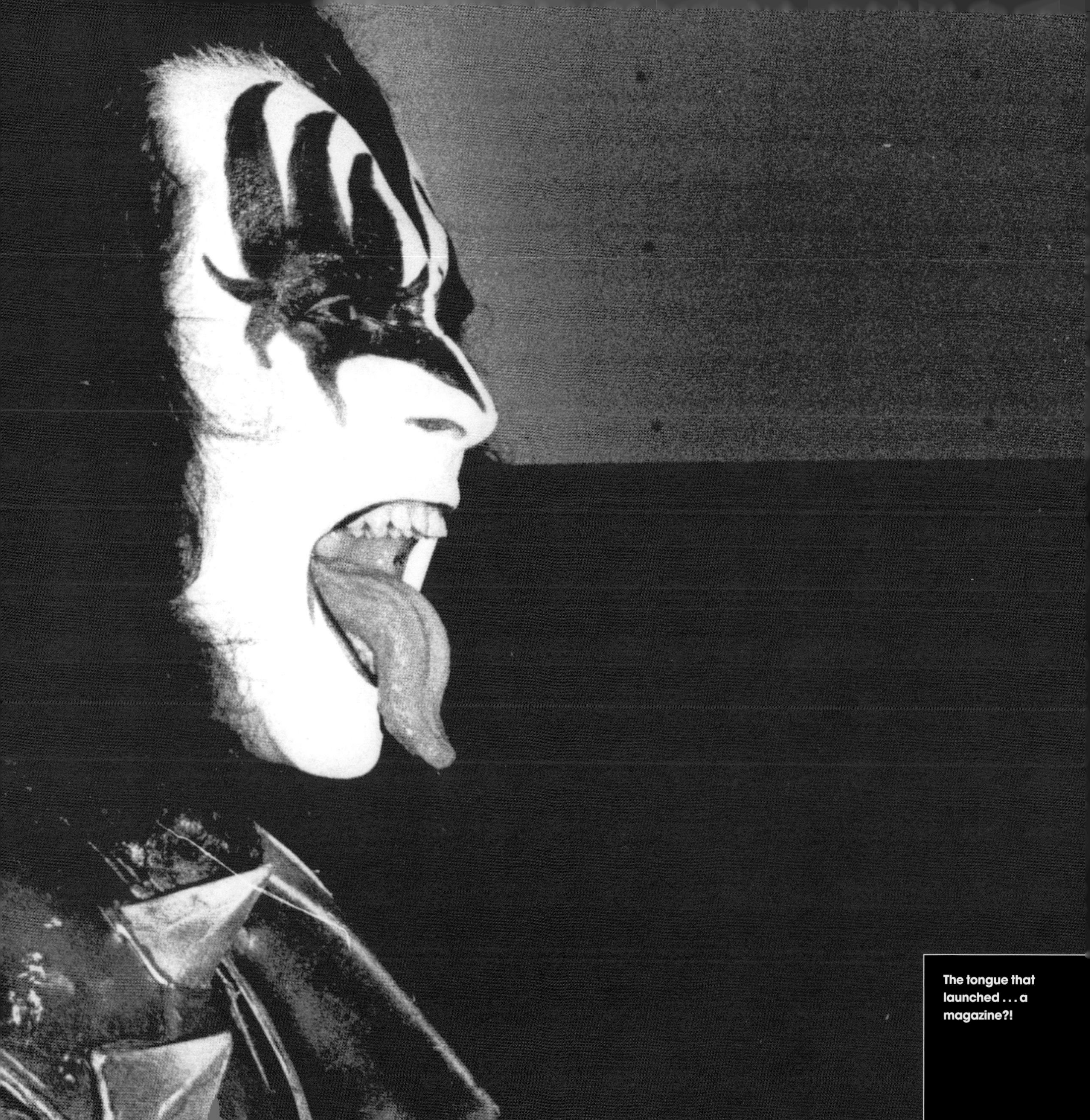

The tongue that launched . . . a magazine?!

AUGUST '76 TOUR DATES

August 2	**Market Square Arena**	**Indianapolis, IN**
August 4	**T.H. Barton Coliseum**	**Little Rock, AR**
August 6	**Roberts Municipal Stadium**	**Evansville, IN**
August 8	**Hara Arena**	**Dayton, OH**
August 10	**Hirsch Coliseum**	**Shreveport, LA**
August 11	**Tarrant County Convention Center**	**Fort Worth, TX**
August 13	**The Summit**	**Houston, TX**
August 15	**County Coliseum**	**El Paso, TX**
August 17	**Tempe Stadium**	**Tempe, AZ**
August 20	**Anaheim Stadium**	**Anaheim, CA**
August 22	**Coliseum Arena**	**Oakland, CA**
August 27	**Greensboro Coliseum**	**Greensboro, NC**
August 29	**Fulton County Stadium**	**Atlanta, GA**

The *Destroyer* campaign continued in Indianapolis, Indiana, on August 2, followed by dates in the Midwest and South.

With the band on a day off between shows, the August 14 issue of *Record World* found David McGee interviewing Bill Aucoin about his management structure, as well as how he's planning to market Starz. With respect to Kiss, Aucoin tells him: "What's starting to happen is something that we really planned about a year and a half ago, and that is that the fans are starting to recognize that the four members of Kiss have really become an entity unto themselves. In fact, a lot of fans just want to see them. I mean, the music is obviously just as ultra-important as everything else in the show, but they're starting to rise above that. They're becoming figures beyond what their show is and beyond what their music is, which is starting to get very exciting.

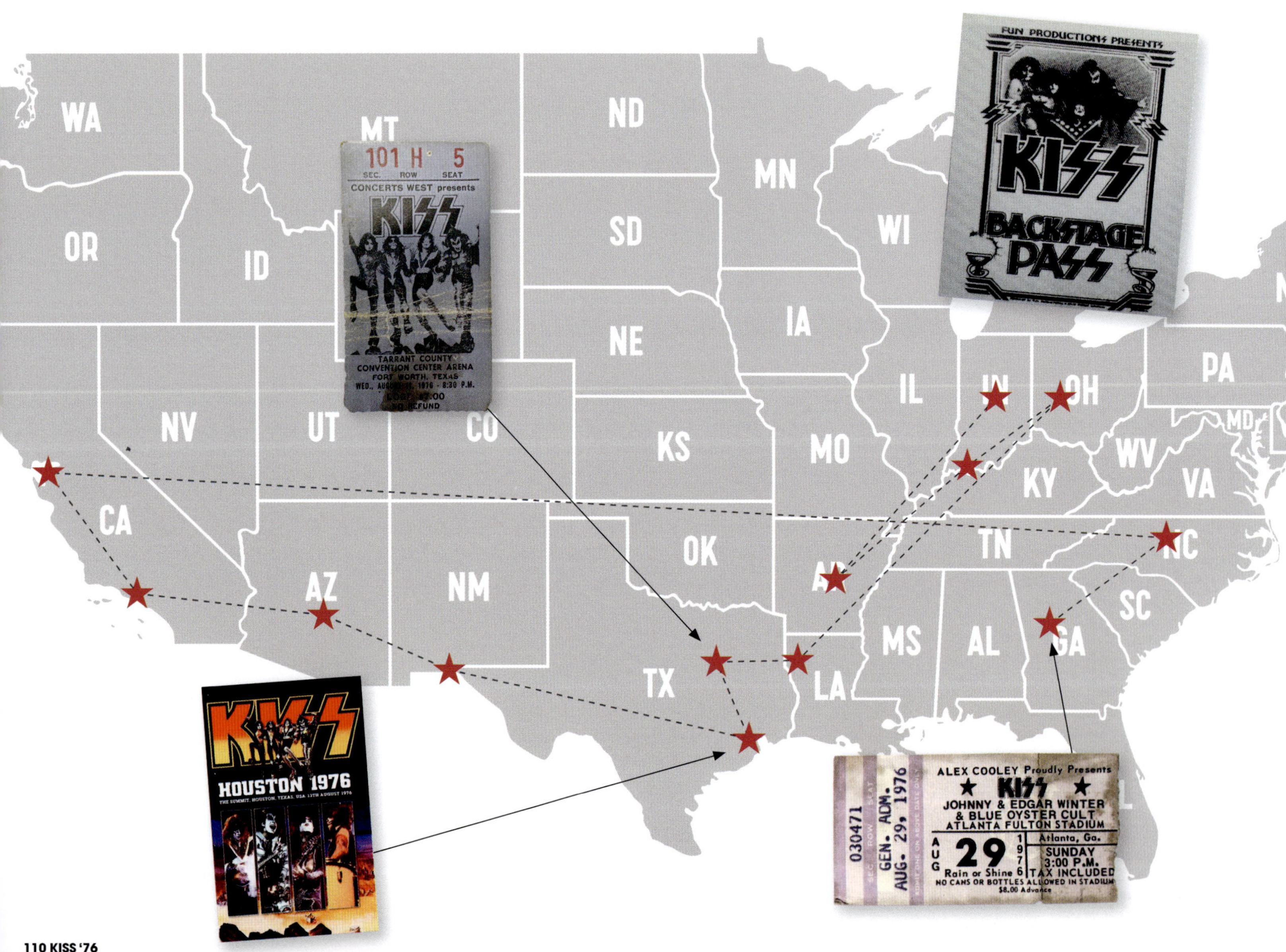

Gene gets his gleeful fanboy hands all over the George Barris collection of custom cars (specifically the *Munster Koach*) in North Hollywood, California, on August 21. The session was for *Creem* magazine, who treated Kiss like a guilty pleasure.

"Right now we're coping with a lot of things. The (Bob) Ezrin album wasn't exactly a total success in my eyes, only because we were trying to take them to the next level, and I think we went too far in that direction. What we did was to follow Bob's avenue—which was a great educational process because he's such a fine producer—but, in fact, I think we went too far. I think at this point we're going to be going back for the next album and make a much stronger rock album instead of trying to go further than that. We might've done a little too much production on the last album."

When McGee asks him whether Kiss should be doing theatrical albums, Aucoin says: "No, I don't. I'm kind of reversing myself on that. That's one of the things that a manager can do, I guess. I'm just not sure we had to go that far. I'm only saying that the fans are so strong in back of Kiss that I think a lot of them wondered why we went that far out. Why did they have to do this? And I don't think that they accepted it easily. There are a few cuts on the album that they really liked, that we got good response on, in fact, but on a lot of the cuts we did too much production. The strong rock fans didn't relate to that. Now Kiss's older audience has related to it, but that's not where we're really centered. We found that we went against our philosophy a little bit in trying to do something new. Which I'm not against. I don't mind trying something new. I just think we went too far. You'll find that the next album, which is going to be produced by Eddie Kramer, is probably going to be closer to a rock album, much, much stronger rock 'n' roll. It's going to be closer to where Kiss really is, I think. I think Bob felt that he was going to be the producer of Kiss. I think that we all did at the time. We just felt that we had gone too far, that we really had to go another way. Also, we got tremendous feedback that a lot of the fans felt that *Destroyer* was too close to (Alice) Cooper. That it was a Bob Ezrin album and not a Kiss album. A strong feedback. I'll bet you that 70 to 80 percent of the feedback was

IN WORLD NEWS...

In August, there were bombings, gun rampages, hijackings, dictators doing dictator things, fires, work-related explosions, plane crashes, and even a tsunami. But if you haven't gathered so far, for the most part, things are being kept relatively light throughout the course of this book.

Back to our regular programming, on August 1, the Seattle Seahawks play their first game, a preseason affair. The Tampa Bay Buccaneers debut this year as well, going 0–14. Also on the same day, Niki Lauda crashes in a Formula One race, suffering severe burns but surviving. The next day, Fritz Lang, producer of *Metropolis*, dies at the age of eighty-five.

This page and following: Rich Galbraith created these heroic-looking live shots at Kansas City, Missouri.

On August 5, London's Big Ben breaks, failing to ring, but then the popular sitcom *What's Happening!!* debuts. Another big opening day takes place on August 10, when the massively popular musical *Annie* debuts off-Broadway. The next day, John Wayne, popular gun-toting hero among many young Kiss fans, appears in his last movie,

The Shootist. In further TV news, on August 30, Tom Brokaw begins his run anchoring NBC's *Today* show, and the next day, another sitcom popular among kids, *Alice,* launches, staring Linda Lavin as a waitress in a diner. But it's Flo, played by Polly Holliday, who coins the catchphrase of the day, when she tells her boss Mel to "Kiss my grits!"

If yelling that when hanging out with your friends wouldn't get a laugh, there was always "Up your nose with a rubber hose" (*Welcome Back, Kotter*), "You big dummy" (*Sanford and Son*), "Dy-no-mite!" (*Good Times*), "Lookin' good!" (*Chico and the Man*), "Sit on it" (*Happy Days*), or a simple "Aaayyyy!" (when swanning into a room, two thumbs up), also from *Happy Days*, made famous by everybody's hero, the Fonz.

Wrapping up, on August 16, the NFL stages its first game ever outside of the United States, with the St. Louis Cardinals beating the San Diego Chargers in Tokyo, Japan. Three days later, Gerald Ford narrowly defeats Ronald Reagan to win the Republican nomination for president.

These boots are made for rocking. Gene takes care of business, despite impractical footwear.

IN MUSIC NEWS...

On August 9, Grand Funk Railroad issue an eleventh studio album. *Good Singin', Good Playin'* is famously produced by Frank Zappa. Like Kiss, Grand Funk issue two albums in 1976. More impressively, Grand Funk worked as hard as Kiss did but a rock 'n' roll generation earlier, issuing five studio albums and a double live album between

1969 and 1971, with everything certifying platinum or higher except for one. Also like Kiss, they issued their double live album after three studio albums.

As popular in the press as Grand Funk, Elton John closes out his tour with seven sold-out dates at Madison Square Garden, commencing August 10. But things are not so

Launch sequence engaged. Ace rockets into space from the Toledo Sports Arena.

good for Keith Moon, who, on the following day, collapses in a Miami hotel room and has to be rushed to hospital.

In punk rock news, on August 14, Stiff Records in the United Kingdom issue their first bit of product, a single from Nick Lowe. Two days later, the Ramones play their first "proper" gig, at CBGB. Also on August 16, France hosts what is widely considered the very first "punk rock festival," featuring the Damned and Eddie and the Hot Rods. Not punk, but another milestone (and also on the same day), Cliff Richard becomes the first western act to perform in the Soviet Union.

On August 21, the Rolling Stones headline a festival bill at Knebworth in the United Kingdom, with an estimated 120,000 fans in attendance. Also on the ticket are Todd Rundgren, 10CC, and Lynyrd Skynyrd, with the southern rockers enjoying a successful 1976 at home as well. Soon to eclipse Skynyrd, Kiss, and just about anybody else, at least in terms of baby bands, is Boston, who issue their self-titled

In support of muscular dystrophy research, Kiss meet fans and sign autographs at a Peaches record story in Atlanta, Georgia, on August 14.

asking why we did a Bob Ezrin album, an Alice Cooper–type thing. Which turned out to be a little bit of a negative. I think the fans feel that Alice is over; at least that was in the minds of the Kiss fans. So we're going to kind of split the difference. We're not going all the way back, but we're certainly going to make a stronger rock 'n' roll album this time out. Straight-ahead."

Also in the same issue of *Record World*, there's a brief missive about the new single, "Detroit Rock City," stating, "America's hard rock heroes show what they do best here with this hard rockin' *Destroyer* cut. Edited down from the LP length, the song is primed for maximum airplay in Detroit or any other rock city."

Also on August 14, Kiss did an in-store appearance at a Peaches Records & Tapes outlet in Atlanta, Georgia. Along with meeting fans and signing autographs, there was a "Kiss Off" campaign in support of muscular dystrophy research, where the band along with Miss Dixie Speedway sold kisses for ninety-three cents, priced for supporting station, Radio Z93.

Touring duties resumed in the Southwest and California, with the band headlining in Anaheim on August 20, supported by Bob Seger, Ted Nugent, and Montrose in front of forty-three thousand fans. All of those bands would have been responsible for a portion of the ticket sales, especially Ted Nugent, whose debut solo band album had just gone gold a month earlier, with *Free for All* reaching that plateau in November. Nugent and Seger actually joined Kiss for multiple shows on this tour leg, as did Artful Dodger.

On August 19, "Beth" was issued as a single, en route to one million in sales in June 1977. Two days later, between landmark shows, Gene conducted a photo shoot for *Creem* magazine, with a hot rod car, at the George Barris Car Collection, North Hollywood, California, again working with Barry Levine.

Back in Atlanta, Georgia, on August 29, was another big one, with thirty-four thousand fans taking in performances by Bob Seger, both Johnny and Edgar Winter, .38 Special, Blue Öyster Cult, and of course Kiss. After the show, when the crew was tearing down, the huge devil cats (wearing crosses) that sit on either side of Peter's drum kit got stolen. Years later, they popped up as Halloween decorations at a house in Atlanta.

debut album on August 26. The album will certify platinum by the end of the year, en route to its current status at seventeen-times platinum. Despite putting out only two albums in the 1970s, Boston will become part of the conversation among the kids with respect to successful US hard rock acts, while also simultaneously leading (by far) a next wave that includes Starz, Angel, and Derringer.

Finally, the big hit songs this month include Elton John's duet with Kiki Dee, "Don't Go Breaking My Heart," along with Wings' "Let 'Em In," ABBA's "Dancing Queen," the Bee Gees' "You Should Be Dancing," and Queen's "You're My Best Friend."

Peter nearly reprises the pose from the cover of *Alive!* The Pearl logo is prominent, Criss having banked a profitable endorsement deal with the drum manufacturer.

SEPTEMBER

Rocking the venerable Hammersmith Odeon, May 15–16. It's not the kind of venue we typically associate with Kiss.

SEPTEMBER '76 TOUR DATES

September 1	**Notre Dame Center**	**South Bend, IN**
September 3	**The Coliseum**	**Richfield, OH**
September 4	**Civic Arena**	**Pittsburgh, PA**
September 6	**Varsity Stadium**	**Toronto, ON**
September 8	**Freedom Hall Coliseum**	**Louisville, KY**
September 10	**Riverfront Coliseum**	**Cincinnati, OH**
September 12	**Springfield Civic Center**	**Springfield, MA**

More important than any shows in late September and into October, Paul, Gene, Ace, and Peter were getting together with Eddie Kramer at the Star Theatre in Nanuet, New York, working on tracks that will compose the band's fifth studio album. The idea was to take the band back to their roots, play pretty much live, or at least on some manner of stage and not in a studio (see feature).

But first there are shows, beginning with South Bend, Indiana, on September 1, and ending with Springfield, Massachusetts, on September 12. Supporting, variously, are Artful Dodger and Bob Seger. The Springfield show represents the end of *The Spirit of '76* tour.

On September 25, *The Originals* reached its *Billboard* chart peak. It would reenter the charts in May 1977. Also on this day, "Beth" reached #7 on the *Billboard* charts.

Over in the press, the September 28 issue of *Circus* included a strident four-page article on the band, titled "Kiss Tour '76: The Ooze of the Greasepaint, The Roar of the Crowd," written by Kathi Stein. There was an ad for *The Originals* on the back cover, and in the Top 20, *Destroyer* was #1 and *Alive!* was #3. The rest of this wonderful chart was a perfect

Paul—not a ham, as he says, but the whole pig. Toledo Sports Arena, July 31, 1976.

rock 'n' roll smorgasbord of all the albums that were important for all of us at the time besides Kiss, namely (and in order, starting at #2), *Rocks, Presence, A Night at the Opera, Frampton Comes Alive!, 2112, Black and Blue, Ted Nugent, Physical Graffiti, Rising, Toys in the Attic, Station to Station, Run with the Pack, Alice Cooper Goes to Hell, Changes One, Fool for the City, We Sold Our Soul for Rock 'n' Roll, Wings at the Speed of Sound,* and *Agents of Fortune*. To reiterate, if you were a thirteen-year-old Kiss fan in 1976, almost all of those were the other new albums you knew. On the cover of the issue was Chevy Chase—of course we all loved *NBC's Saturday Night* (live) as well.

Creem put Rod Stewart on the cover of its September issue, but Kiss is there in large type, as in "Kiss Blitz London." When you get to the article on page 53, it's one page and mostly filled with four pictures.

A survey of the gear the band used appeared in the September issue of *Hit Parader*. There was also a short bit in the Rock & Roll Hotline section, with Lisa Robinson writing, "Gene said that in Harrisburg, Pennsylvania, a group of religious fanatics surrounded the hall outside a Kiss concert chanting, 'Get the devil out of Harrisburg!' 'I guess they thought I was the devil,' marveled Gene, who couldn't be sweeter."

Quipped Gene, "Whenever anyone writes a bad article on us, the kids bring it to the show and burn it in front of us." Adds Lisa, "Marvel Comics writer Steve Gerber (he does *Howard the Duck*) saw Kiss for the first time in Toronto last month before he began work on the special Kiss comic book. And screenplays are still being considered for Kiss's first film project. When the band returns from their first European and English tour (she is writing this in May), they will rehearse in an airplane hanger for their US summer dates. For those dates, Kiss will employ all new costumes, stage effects, staging, and show concept. This should be something."

IN WORLD NEWS...

On September 5, *The Muppet Show*, pride and joy of Jim Henson, premieres but in the United Kingdom as a UK production. Joel Grey guests. Of course, Kiss fans in 1976 were raised on *Sesame Street*.

On September 9 the VHS recording format is introduced at a press conference in Tokyo by Japan Victor Corporation, a conglomerate that includes Kiss's record label in Japan. On September 17, NASA announces the shuttle program.

Back to TV, from September 12 to 28, *Happy Days* reaches its peak of popularity with the "Fonzie Loves Pinky" episodes. It's a toss-up who was cooler in 1976, Kiss or the Fonz.

A triumphant display of Gene breathing fire, California 1976.

On September 22, detective show *Charlie's Angels* debuts, featuring three attractive ladies—Farrah Fawcett, Kate Jackson, and Jacyln Smith—beating up bad guys. More important to Kiss fans was the famous poster of 29-year-old Fawcett in a red swimsuit, first sold in 1976. It moved over six million copies in its first year, and at twelve million sold to date, it's considered the biggest-selling poster of all time. Young Kiss fans also flock to a new TV series, first aired on September 6, about ancient mysteries and conspiracy theories. *In Search of . . .* starred Leonard Nimoy, already big with kids through *Star Trek*.

Also on TV is the first US presidential debate since 1960, aired live on September 23, pitting Gerald Ford against Jimmy Carter. A better fight takes place five days later when Muhammad Ali meets Ken Norton for the third time, coming to blows at Madison Square Garden, with Ali winning by decision. Kiss's last show ever was at the same venue, considered their home arena, December 2, 2023.

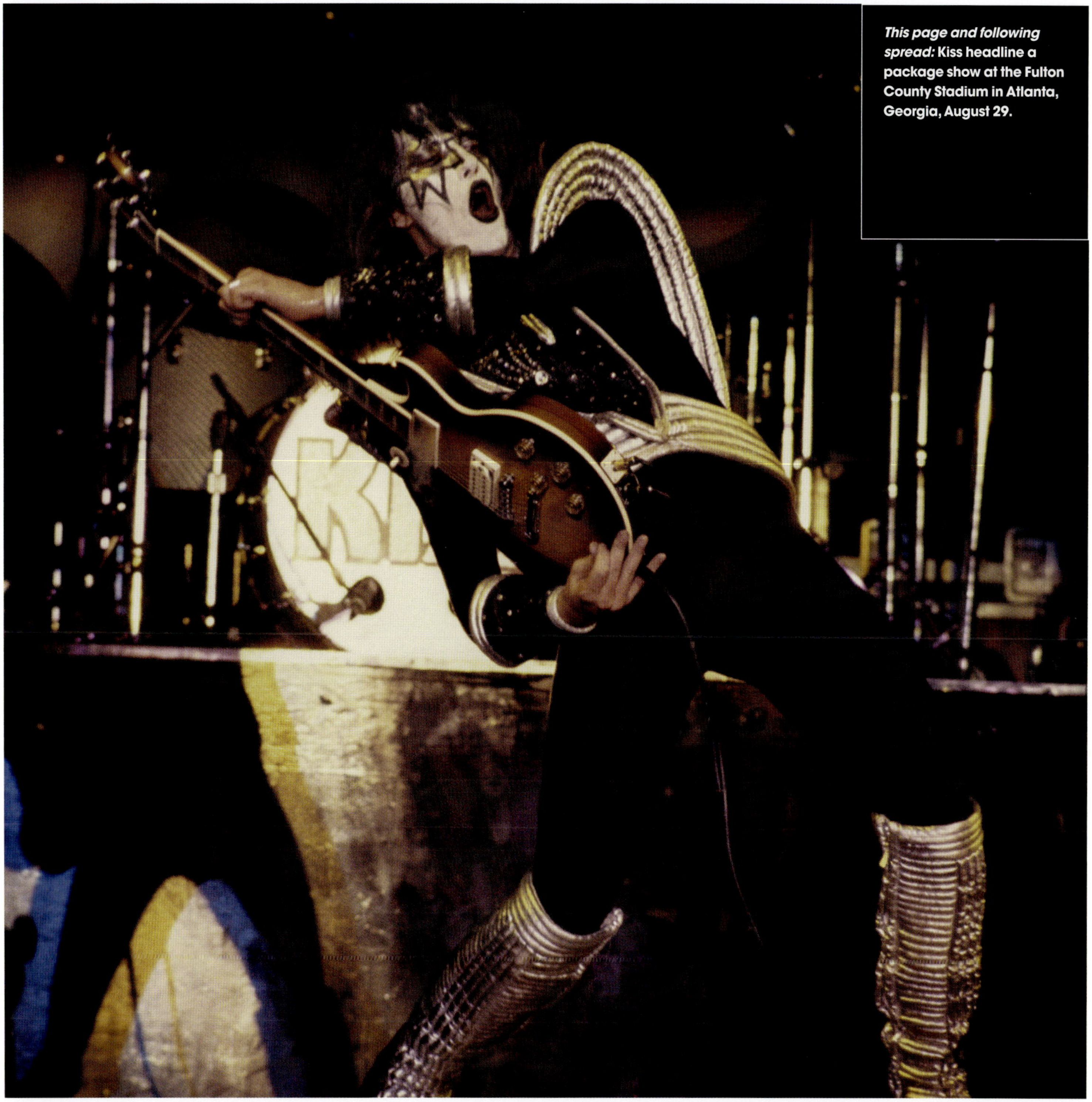

This page and following spread: Kiss headline a package show at the Fulton County Stadium in Atlanta, Georgia, August 29.

IN MUSIC NEWS...

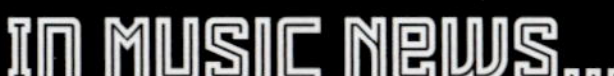

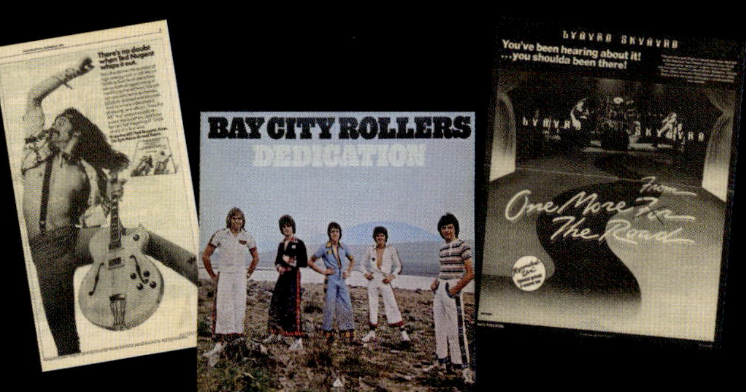

Ted Nugent issues *Free for All*, which notches gold before the end of the year, while the Bay City Rollers issue *Dedication*, which notches gold in November 1977. Montrose issue *Jump on It*, with the band supporting Kiss sporadically. Canadian rockers April Wine come out with *The Whole World's Goin' Crazy*, but they won't swim in the same waters as Kiss

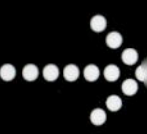

until the early 1980s. Certainly on Kiss's level already is Lynyrd Skynyrd, who issue *One More from the Road*, which eventually goes triple platinum. On September 29, Rush issue *All the World's a Stage*, a double live album after four studio albums, somewhat mirroring Kiss's strategy. On September 13, the Bee Gees issue their fourteenth album,

Children of the World, which goes platinum, fueled by "You Should Be Dancing." On September 17, Ringo Starr returns with *Rotogravure*, and the next day, Stevie Wonder gives us *Songs in the Key of Life*.

The September 8 edition of *Rolling Stone* contains an interview with Elton John, where he opens up about his bisexuality. On September 14, Bob Dylan has NBC air his *Hard Rain* concert special to coincide with the live album of the same name.

On September 18, Queen prove their ascendance with a free concert in Hyde Park to 150,000 fans. Also proving their worth, at the Rock Music Awards on CBS, Fleetwood Mac win best group and album,

while Peter Frampton is deemed Rock Personality of the Year.

A couple days later, there's the landmark 100 Club Punk Festival in London. Playing September 20 and 21 are the Clash, the Sex Pistols, the Buzzcocks, and the Damned, among others, with Siouxsie and the Banshees performing live for the very first time. Punk would never be much of a bother to Kiss. They were too busy fulfilling the demands placed upon them by Neil Bogart and Bill Aucoin to worry about smaller acts or the considerable number of bands doing as well or better than them. Another act keeping folks employed at the label was Parliament, who see their *Mothership Connection* album certify platinum on September 20.

On September 25, in Dublin, a band called Feedback is born, soon to become U2. Three days later, AC/DC finally have an album released in North America, entitled *High Voltage*. On September 29, Jerry Lee Lewis shoots his bass player, Butch Owens, in the chest. Owens survives to fight another day.

OCTOBER

Ace, once more clutching a classic Gibson Les Paul sunburst, his steadfast choice of weapon and one that many of his personal musical heroes also employed.

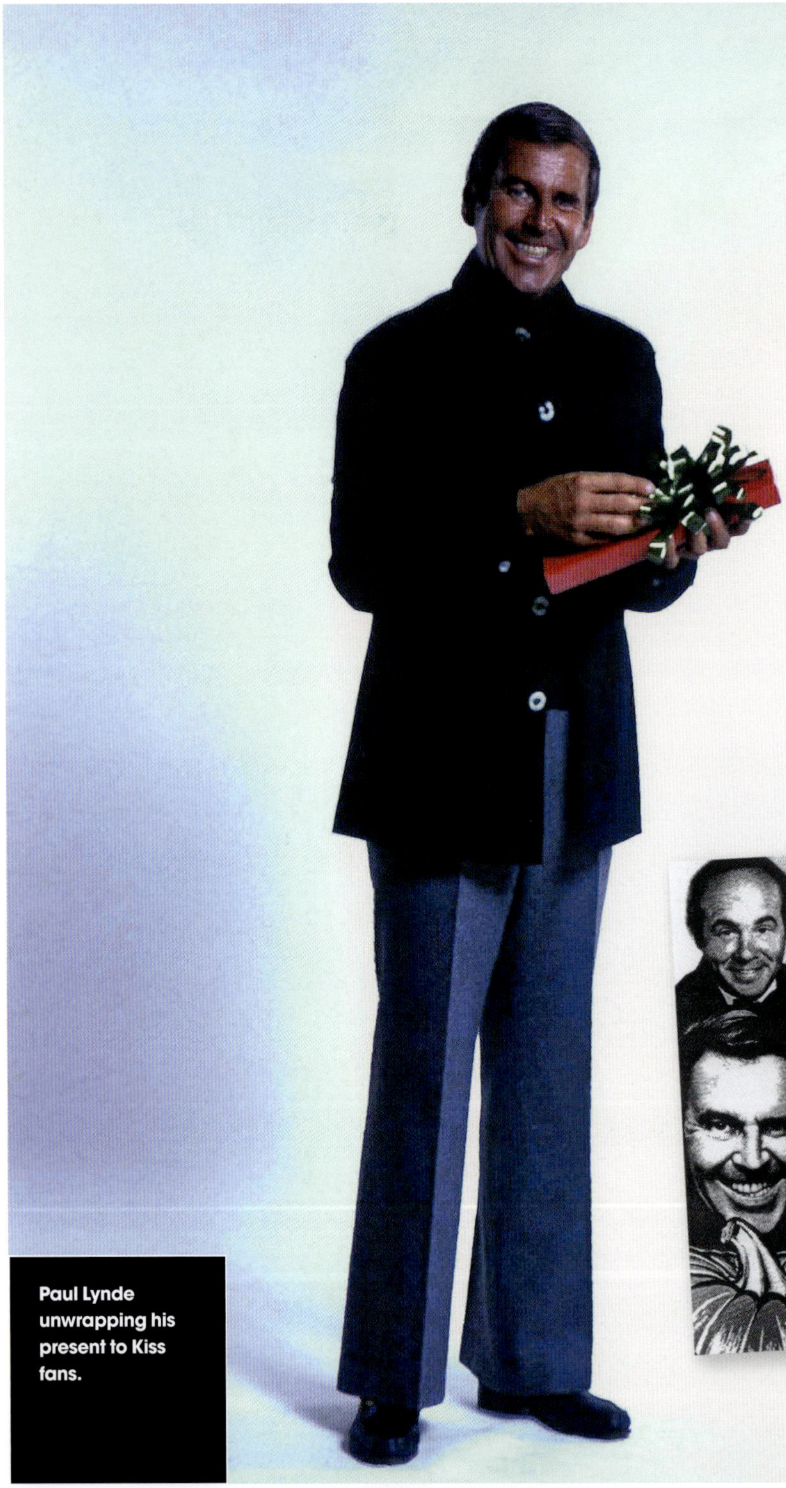

On October 2, after drifting off the charts, *Destroyer* climbed back on, at #133, reaching the peak of this second wind in May 1977. On October 19, the band are working at Rehearsal Hall #5 at ABC Studios in Hollywood, California, in advance of their appearance on *The Paul Lynde Halloween Special*, to be aired on October 29. Manager Bill Aucoin was skeptical about putting the band on TV, but it turned out to be one of the key media triumphs ever for Kiss, a vivid memory from 1976 for any young fan of the band. The band and Paul Lynde, genuinely funny, put the show to tape on the following two days, with "Detroit Rock City" being recorded on October 20 and "Beth" and "King of the Night Time World" recorded on October 21, along with some final skit acting and a credits sequence. Also memorable in their performances were Margaret Hamilton, reprising her role as the Wicked Witch of the West, and *H.R. Pufnstuf*'s Witchiepoo, played by Billie Hayes.

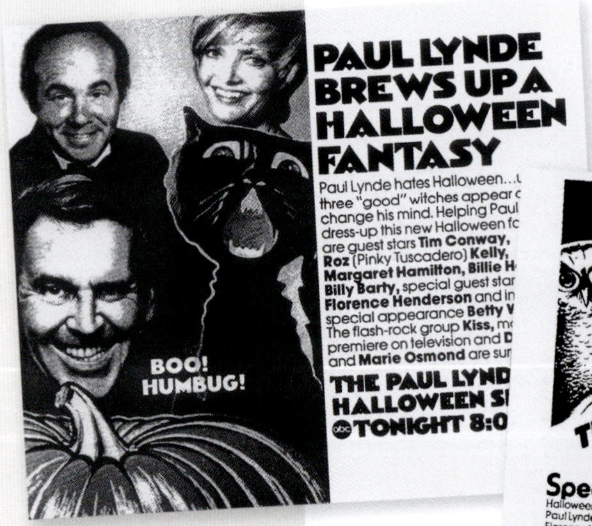

Paul Lynde unwrapping his present to Kiss fans.

PAUL LYNDE BREWS UP A HALLOWEEN FANTASY
Paul Lynde hates Halloween...
three "good" witches appear
change his mind. Helping Paul
dress-up this new Halloween
are guest stars **Tim Conway,**
Roz (Pinky Tuscadero) **Kelly,**
Margaret Hamilton, Billie H
Billy Barty, special guest star
Florence Henderson and in
special appearance **Betty**
The flash-rock group **Kiss,**
premiere on television and
and **Marie Osmond** are sur
BOO! HUMBUG!
THE PAUL LYND
HALLOWEEN S
abc TONIGHT 8:0

IN WORLD NEWS...

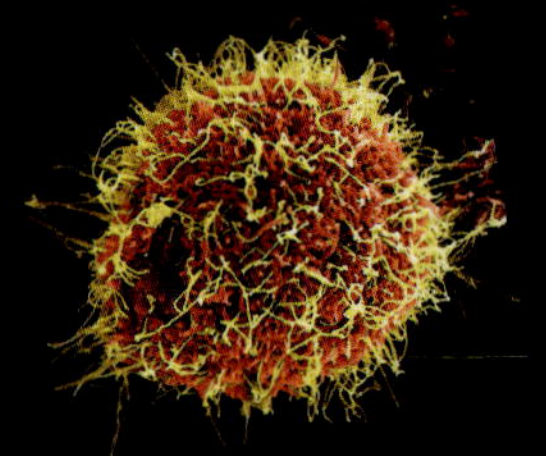

On October 4, the United States lifts its ban on the death penalty, and a week later the Ebola virus is identified for the first time by microscope. On October 15, the Bermuda Triangle strikes again, when a Brazilian cargo ship is lost at sea, along with its crew of thirty-seven. Also on October 15, Americans witness the first debate between prospective vice presidents, when Walter Mondale and Bob Dole go at it in Houston.

On October 18, Ford begins production of the Fiesta, their tiniest car yet, to combat the Japanese, who are kicking the American car industry's collective butts at this time with Toyotas and Datsuns. On October 21, the Cincinnati Reds

Peter Criss transforms into the Catman while his lion-tamer wife Lydia looks on. The two were married from 1970 to 1978.

sweep the New York Yankees to win the World Series, with Reds catcher Johnny Bench being a hero with the kids at that time. Three days later, the United Kingdom's James Hunt narrowly wins the Formula One World Championship. But perhaps most important sports-wise to a Kiss fan in 1976 is Evel Knievel jumping seven Greyhound buses on Halloween at the Seattle Kingdome. This was Knievel in his twilight years but still absolutely massive of legend.

But the slide for Knievel couldn't be stopped. Inspired by the hit movie *Jaws*, he was supposed to jump a tank of sharks three months later but, during rehearsal, crashed into cameraman Thomas Geren,

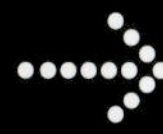

"I want you!" Paul Stanley backstage in Los Angeles.

permanently injuring Geren's eye, which devasted Knievel, resulting in a cancellation of his jump scheduled for the next day. Later, in 1977, when Fonzie jumps a shark on water skis on an episode of *Happy Days*, fans collectively roll their eyes, giving birth to the expression "jumping the shark."

IN MUSIC NEWS ...

Big records this month include Robin Trower's *Long Misty Days*, which goes gold, following up *Live!* from earlier in 1976. By this point, there's a bit of a battle for guitar hero rights going on between Robin Trower, Ted Nugent, and Frank Marino of Mahogany Rush fame. Ace isn't really part of the conversation, and neither are Joe Perry and Brad Whitford, suffering somewhat by

Also on October 19, besides rehearsal, the band squeezed in a *Creem* magazine photo shoot with Neil Preston, who put the band in a winter scene, covered in snow, working at A&M Records, also in Hollywood. The fake snow used turned out to be quite toxic, and it was found in the company's ventilation system for months afterward. Even worse, Ace was highly intoxicated and fell over face down into the "snow" and began coughing up blood. He was quickly whisked away before anybody could force him to go to the hospital.

In the October issue of *Hit Parader*, Richard Robinson reflected, "During the past year I've gotten to know Peter, Gene, Paul, and Ace, it's become obvious to me that they are presently the top live rock 'n' roll band in America. Like Grand Funk Railroad and Alice Cooper before them, this band has a certain energy and appeal that will never be understood by those who don't believe in rock 'n' roll. They are the current incarnation of rock as phenomenon. My knowledge of them as people gives me the impression that if they keep at it, they can only get bigger."

When Robinson asked Peter about the transformation that happens when he puts on the makeup, Peter says, "It's the mystique. I get into the part of being a drummer. Drums are just so hostile. Lions are so freaky. I love cats. I always did. I had this cat and I was just staring at him one night and I said, boy, that's freaky. I started to draw a sketch of him. I drew the cat's head on a body and said that would really be weird and I came up with that image for me."

But he's trying to stay grounded. Peter says: "I've always felt that you have to cry to really know how to laugh. I believe that. You have to feel that way in life because the people you are going to meet on the way up, you are going to meet on the way down. It took me a long time to get here. I paid my dues my way. I wanna keep it, man. Kiss isn't my whole life. It isn't to me, because I have my lady and I really love her a lot and if it all fell through tomorrow, we'd still have each other. I need Kiss, you know; I've got to have music, man. Music is what I'm surviving on. But I don't live on it 24 hours a day. I meet musicians who do it as a 24-hour thing, but if you do that and really believe the writeups, you'll go crazy. That's my outlook.

"We're each going through our own trip. But we're dealing with it. There's some groups that get crazy and ego comes in and chicks come in and money comes in and then they blow it. And it isn't the same once you blow it. To make it you've got to keep the chemistry right. I mean you could put a new guy up there to replace any one of us and the kids would know it. They'd feel it—I don't care if he played lick for lick. Kiss is right as it is and I'm glad that we're really together. We really like one another and we respect one another and that's important."

Says Paul on his own makeup, "More than a character, I was looking for a feel. I didn't sit down and say I'm going to be the so-and-so or this, and I'm not going to be a cat. I was more into an attitude. And a vibe, a feel. I'm as comfortable with makeup as without. It only reaffirms for me what I am. Just like clothes."

The *Creem* cover and advertisement that resulted from Neal Preston's October 19 photo shoot with the band.

having to split the praise, not to mention by being part of a band and not sort of a solo artist like those other guys. New on the scene are Rick Derringer and Pat Travers as well, joining the fight—and there's always Ronnie Montrose, too, not to mention old guard institutions like Jimmy Page. Same split or division of votes happens with Brian Robertson and Scott Gorham from Thin Lizzy, who issue *Johnny the Fox* this month. Also, Styx issue *Crystal Ball*, their first with Tommy Shaw, and Black Oak Arkansas cap off a busy 1976, which produces two studio albums and a live album. October's offering is *10 Yr Overnight Success*.

In the United Kingdom, on October 8, the Sex Pistols sign a record deal with EMI, and in Canada, power trio Triumph issue their self-titled debut album. Now there is Rush, Triumph, and Moxy, with Bachman-Turner Overdrive and April Wine on the wane. Right from the beginning, Triumph put together an expensive stage show with lots of lights and pyro that clearly is influenced by the path to

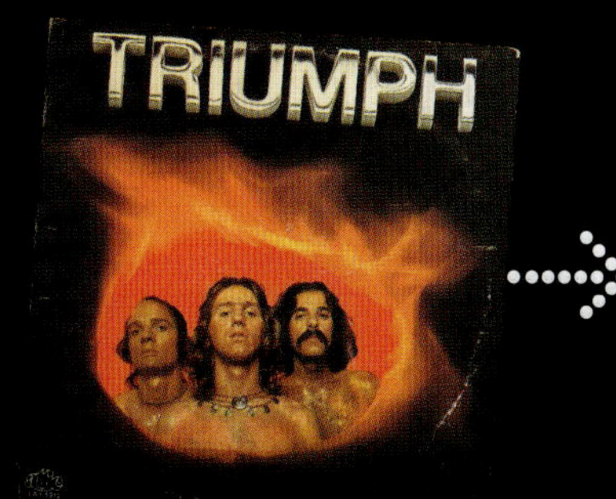

"I love cats . . . I drew the cat's head on a body and said that would really be weird and I came up with that image for me." Peter gets into his part backstage . . .

success paved by Kiss. And their drummer can sing, too.

On October 19, Parliament score a gold album with *The Clones of Dr. Funkenstein*. Parliament, Donna Summer, and Kiss are the acts selling any appreciable amount of records for Casablanca at the time, soon to be joined by Village People and Cher, with Cher and Gene being an item for a couple of years. On October 20, Led Zeppelin's *The Song Remains the Same* film debuts, with the double live album to follow two days later. Also on a busy October 22, Black Sabbath issue their seventh studio album, *Technical Ecstasy*, and the Damned issue "New Rose," the first UK punk single ever. In addition, Elton John issues his eleventh studio album, *Blue Moves*, and Bob Seger issues his breakthrough *Night Moves* album, with Seger having supported Kiss on many of the *Destroyer* tour dates.

A lone American progressive rock band finds its way to success, when on October 21, Kansas issue *Leftoverture*. Fueled by the smash hit status of the multipart

. . . meanwhile, Gene fully embraces his "Demon" persona onstage at the Los Angeles Forum.

"Carry On Wayward Son," the album eventually sells four-times platinum. Five days hence, Kiss's crosstown rivals Blue Öyster Cult have their own hit with "(Don't Fear) the Reaper." Somewhat of a ballad, it's pretty much BÖC's version of "Beth," driving *Agents of Fortune* to a gold certification on October 26.

Finally, on Halloween, Parliament begin the *P-Funk/ Rubber Band Earth* tour, in Houston, Texas. Taking cue from Kiss, the Casablanca conglomerate put on an elaborate costume-festooned show, which includes a "mother ship" that would deliver the band to the stage.

JANUARY
FEBRUARY
MARCH
APRIL
MAY
JUNE
JULY
AUGUST
SEPTEMBER
OCTOBER

NOVEMBER

DECEMBER

A confident Kiss in their element, helped to that place by photographer and consummate pro Fin Costello.

NOVEMBER '76 TOUR DATES

November 24	**Civic Center**	**Savannah, GA**
November 25	**Charlotte Coliseum**	**Charlotte, NC**
November 27	**J.S. Dorton Arena**	**Raleigh, NC**
November 28	**Memorial Auditorium**	**Greenville, SC**
November 30	**Municipal Auditorium**	**Columbus, GA**

With a new album called *Rock and Roll Over* in the can, Kiss celebrated with a new single on the first day of the month called "Hard Luck Woman." Then comes a series of tour rehearsal sessions, first at SIR in New York, from November 7 to 12, and then at the Reading Armory, Camp Curtis Guild, in Reading, Massachusetts, from November 15 to 21, with these classified as dress rehearsals.

In the meantime, the new album comes out on November 11, shipping gold. Also on this day, *Destroyer* goes platinum and Ted Nugent's *Free for All* goes gold. In Reading on November 21, the band shot videos for use on an upcoming episode of *Don Kirshner's Rock Concert*, to be aired on May 28, 1977. The three tracks chosen—"Hard Luck Woman," "I Want You," and "Love 'Em and Leave 'Em"—would demonstrate the range of the new album (i.e., ballad, heavy metal song, and something in the middle like the old days).

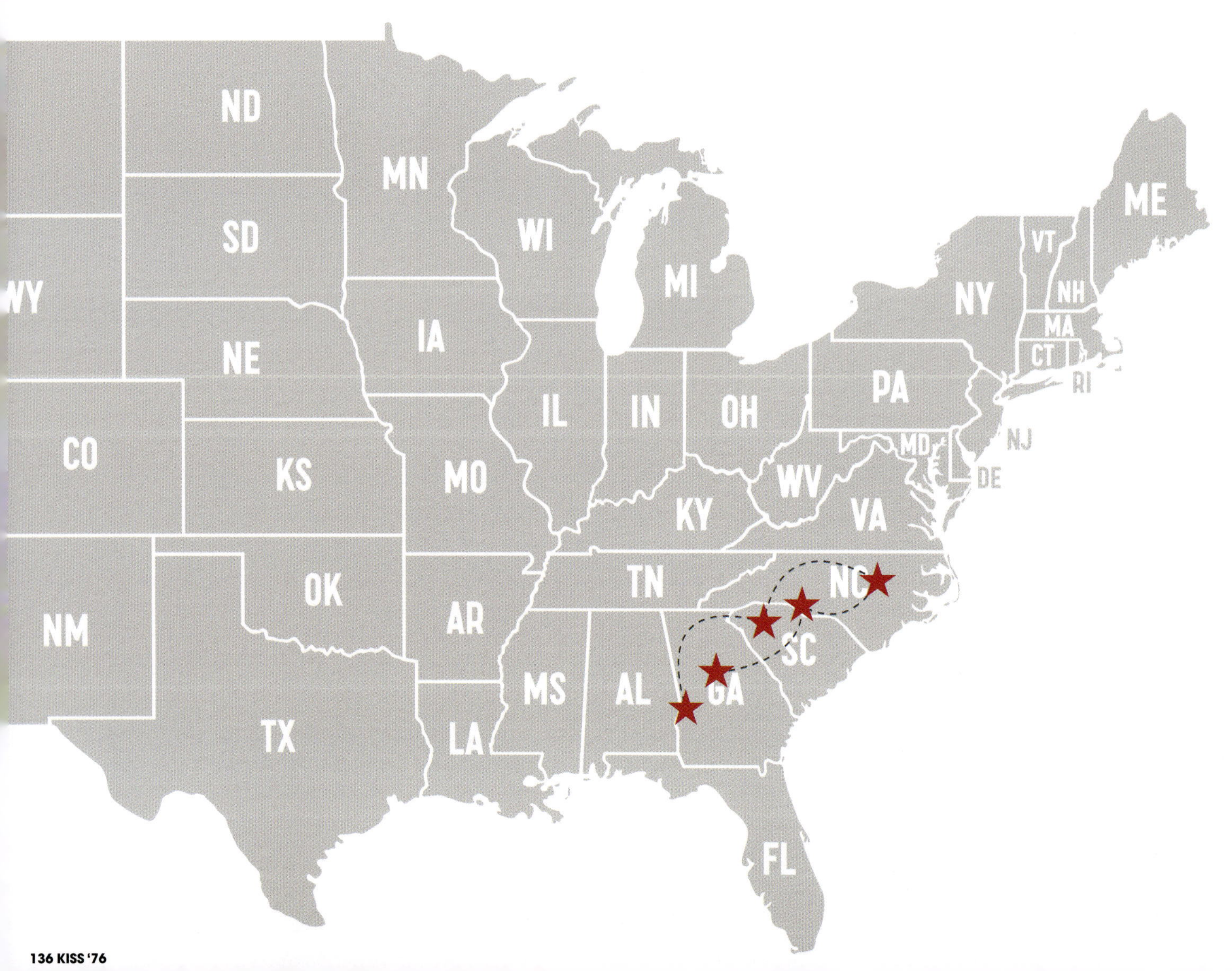

"Hey, let's make another record!" Kiss kicked off November with the new single "Hard Luck Woman" off their new LP.

On November 20, *Record World* announces, "A concerted effort has been made here to move back to the cruder, raunchier sound of the band's first three sets. Producer Eddie Kramer has helped effect the change via 'See You in Your Dreams,' 'Hard Luck Woman,' and 'Ladies Room.' Continued improvement in playing and writing must also be noted."

The band's first show on their *Winter Tour 1976–1977* in support of *Rock and Roll Over* was in Savannah, Georgia, on November 24. Supporting were Graham Parker and the Rumour, promoting their critically acclaimed *Heat Treatment* album. Notably, Peter sang "Beth" for the first time in a concert setting. The month came to a close in Columbus, Georgia, on November 30, with the aforementioned Tom Petty and the Heartbreakers supporting.

The November 27 issue of *Cash Box* included an elaborate four-page ad spread from Casablanca that states, "Thanks for a golden two years. We're dependent on you." Included are thumbnails of various Kiss, Parliament, and Donna Summer albums, plus the Johnny Carson show excerpts album that certified gold but didn't recoup on its $1.2 million promotional campaign.

There was also a news piece that outlined the band's accomplishments this year: "When 1976 ends and music industry and journalistic pundits withdraw to determine which artist or artists most dramatically dominated the collective attention of audiences during the past 12 months, they will be hard-pressed to ignore the amazing feats accomplished by the bizarrely garbed, outrageously theatrical band called Kiss. In addition to receiving two certified gold album awards, for *Destroyer* and the recently released *Rock and Roll Over* and a

Continued on page 140

IN WORLD NEWS...

On November 2, Jimmy Carter wins the race to become US president. The next day, horror film *Carrie*, starring Sissy Spacek and based on a Stephen King book, debuts in theaters. It becomes a cultural phenomenon and ignites debate about bullying in schools. Or at least people started thinking about it more. The film definitely freaks out Kiss fans and, likely more pointedly,

girls in middle school and high school. Bottom line, *Carrie* is a big deal. The movie gets its major rollout on November 16.

On November 7, *Gone with the Wind* appears for the first time on network television. People forget that many of these classic films were sidelined, waiting for this kind of thing to happen. Airing on NBC over two nights, it garners a 65 percent audience share.

A fantastic "boots first" shot from Fin Costello. Note the guardian cats next to Peter's kit.

On November 12, Ballantine Books publishes *Star Wars: From the Adventures of Luke Skywalker*. When the movie emerges in 1977, it will become direct multimedia competition for the likes of Kiss or indeed anybody selling rock 'n' roll products.

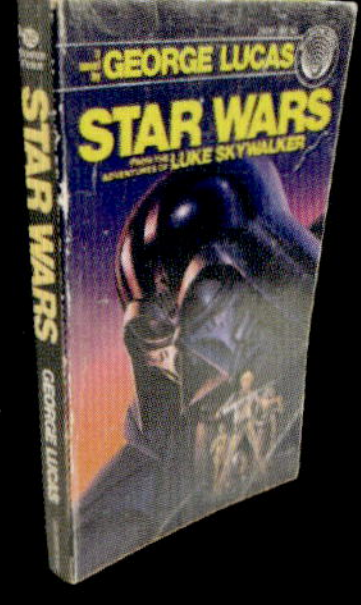

If *Star Wars* mania was still six months away, interest in all things related to King Tutankhamun is on deck right now. On November 17, the National Galley executes a seven-city tour displaying artifacts and telling the mysterious story. Ten million tickets are sold. In 1978, Steve Martin will get in on the act, penning a hit song called "King Tut."

In museum-related news, the next day, November 18, renowned French photographer Man Ray dies at the age of eighty-six. Three days later, *Rocky*, starring Sylvester Stallone, premieres in theaters. Kiss fans, already inspired by Muhammad Ali and other superstar contenders, have a new reason to knock the daylights out of each other.

On November 26, the Microsoft trademark is registered in the state

Peter and his Pearl-y whites. It was a big kit, yet he remained a single-bass-drum guy.

of New Mexico. Home computers and, more importantly for the young Kiss fan, computer games increasingly become part of the suite of entertainment choices. But for those still glued to their television, two days later there's *The Brady Bunch Variety Hour*, marking a reunion for a show that had gone off the air two years earlier. Successful as a special, it would become a weekly go-to called *The Brady Bunch Hour*.

Finally in world events (that a young Kiss fan might follow), on November 29, the Yankees sign Reggie Jackson to what at the time was seen as a stratospheric contract, specifically five years at around $3.5 million.

certified platinum album award for *Destroyer*, a single, 'Beth,' recently completed a three-week stay on the Cash Box Top 100 chart, peaking at #7. Yet, that is only half the story. Kiss presently has four albums on the Cash Box Top 200 Albums chart: *Rock and Roll Over* at #59 with a bullet after two weeks; *The Originals* at #122 after 14 weeks; *Destroyer* at #123 after 29 weeks; and *Alive!* at #126 after 60 weeks."

Noted in *Hit Parader*: "Kiss continues to grow as an American rock phenomenon. The recent release of their first three albums as a triple album set and the platinum status of their live album has convinced many music businesspeople that Kiss won't be stopped. The band are taking all these predictions in their stride. They are intent upon making a valid contribution to rock 'n' roll and while they want to continue to grow, they aren't getting carried away by their incredible success. 'I went to see King Kong. That did it for me. I didn't want to be just a human being walking around in a regular suit,' says Gene Simmons, Kiss bassist and god of hell fire. The rest of the band seems to feel the same. The result: a long summer tour and talk of a Kiss movie and Kiss comic book in the fall."

Paul, all smeared lipstick and Flying V.

IN MUSIC NEWS...

This month, Deep Purple issue a posthumous live album, called *Made in Europe*, putting the wraps on one of the old guard. Also, from the same streets in Manhattan that Kiss knew so well, Lou Reed issues *Rock and Roll Heart*. More adjacent musically, fulfilling the wishes of the "blue jean army" of fans inclined to like Kiss and Aerosmith, Foghat issue *Night Shift*, which includes hit single "Drivin' Wheel" as its opening track—of course, Kiss opened *Destroyer* with a "driving" song as well, and *Rock and Roll Over* contains a song called "Baby Driver." Also this month, David Cassidy issues a third album, called *Getting It in the Street*. *The Partridge Family*, over in 1974 after a ninety-six-

ROCK AND ROLL OVER

THE SESSIONS

"*Destroyer* was an experiment," remarked Paul at the time, in conversation with *Hit Parader*'s Lisa Robinson. "I can listen to it and I'm very pleased with it musically. But it doesn't really show where we're at. After we did three or four albums of one type of music, we wanted a little diversion. The problem was that some people thought that *Destroyer* was the direction we were going in—that the album after *Destroyer* would have us with the Boston Pops or something. But *Rock and Roll Over* is back to the old stuff.

"*Destroyer* is a platinum album. I mean, you can't sneeze at that. Who can sneeze at a platinum album? It's just that, that's not what I ever wanted to achieve. It's Bob Ezrin's album. What we needed at that point was a catalyst. We needed somebody to spur us on. I was a little stagnant at that point in terms of writing and I needed a rest and I needed a shot in the arm at the same time, so we needed someone to direct us. But it was quite . . . you know, it's not a true Kiss album. There are sentiments on it that are Kiss, but the new album is Kiss."

Back to the positive, Paul says, "We learned a lot from doing *Destroyer*, in terms of discipline, and really learning to put our minds to playing and by doing that you play better. I think I've become more and more conscious of the technical side of our music. I can only speak for me. I listen to what we do critically, I think what it's lacking and what I can add. I practice. I practice almost every day. Ultimately, you're judged by your music because when you're no longer performing, people are going to listen to your records and that's ultimately where you leave your mark."

As Paul explained to me in 2005, with respect to the second album of 1976, he aligns it more so with 1977's *Love Gun* than *Destroyer* from earlier in the year. "I think they're very similar. They followed each other very naturally. I think that sometimes we can make a conscious effort to regain something that was on a previous album, and if that album was too long ago, the chances are that we may . . . that it will be a noble attempt, but you're too far past it to actually go back to it. The fact that *Love Gun* and *Rock and Roll Over* followed each other, and were done at a certain point in our career, where things were pretty much status quo from one to the other, makes for them to be similar and consistent. I think they're both really great Kiss albums."

episode run, is in regular reruns and is still beloved by young Kiss fans. The debut *Rex* album, featuring future TV and film star Rex Smith, comes out this month as well. Rex were managed by Leber Krebs, and their self-titled debut was produced by Jack Douglas. They sounded like a cross between Aerosmith, Starz, and Kiss.

On November 9, Tom Petty and the Heartbreakers issue their self-titled debut, and four days later, Scottish hard rock veterans Nazareth issue *Play 'n' the Game*—there's the new guard and the old guard in action, with Kiss somewhere in-between. On November 18, Shagrath from Norwegian black metal act Dimmu Borgir is born. Dimmu Borgir would be known

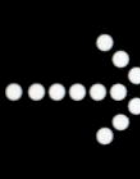

Is Gene off making movies? Wait, it's not the '80s yet!

for their "corpse paint," an update on what Kiss were doing. Also on that day, ex–Tower of Power vocalist Rick Stevens is convicted on murder charges.

On November 19, George Harrison issues *Thirty Three & 1/3*, which goes gold. To promote it, he goes on *NBC's Saturday Night* (live), performing with Paul

Simon. Not exactly headline news, on November 22, the Scorpions issue *Virgin Killer*. They support Kiss on a few European *Destroyer* dates, at which point they would have been touring the previous *In Trance* album. Unknowns now, in 1982 and 1983 they'll be bigger than Kiss. The next day, Thin Lizzy are forced to cancel their US tour when raucous guitarist Brian "Robbo" Robertson slices up his hand in a bar fight, defending Frankie Miller. The band's trajectory looked very much like Kiss's, but escapades like this would end up blunting Lizzy's progress. In the same spirit and on the same day, The Killer, Jerry Lee Lewis, is taken in by cops for drunkenly waving a gun around at

Putting the *Destroyer* experience in the rearview mirror, beginning September 30, 1976, and ending October 16, Kiss reunited with producer Eddie Kramer, who worked with the guys in the thousand-seat in-the-round Star Theatre in Nanuet, New York, ever so slightly upstate from the city. The band was situated on the sunken stage with amplifiers pointed out to the seating area. Kramer set up in an ancillary room and communicated with the band via a video link. The idea was to get some degree of echo, of live ambience, and they experimented by sending a member of the band down a hallway to get even more echo. The band also had the Record Plant truck at their disposal.

Ace was certainly happier with the arrangement. Both he and Peter formed a bloc that wanted this back-to-basics approach, and Ace, recently married, was over the moon that they were recording fifteen minutes from his house. Paul and Gene seemed like they could go either way, having better memories of *Destroyer*. The band had, in fact, asked Aerosmith's producer Jack Douglas to do it, but Jack was friends with Ezrin and told him about the invite, which blew up in the band's face, souring relations with Ezrin. In later years, there was a sense of regret. Paul even frames the reversion to type that *Rock and Roll Over* represented as "chickenshit and a matter of self-preservation." He also thought the sound got smaller when it should have got bigger, to compete with the other heavy bands, in particular Led Zeppelin. And you get the sense from Gene that part of the reason to strip it back was simply to keep the band together, to keep Ace and Peter happy. Gene also admits that *Destroyer* has aged better than these other records.

At times, Peter was also connected to the proceedings by video, with his kit set up in the bathroom. This suited him fine. He was glad to be alone, and he kept himself entertained by doodling pictures and sticking them up in front of the camera pointed at him.

Ace says he and Kramer got along well, which is why he was also the producer of choice on Ace's 1978 solo album. Ace appreciated the fact that Kramer would take him around to pawn shops and pick up different amps to test out. But as Ace told the author, "My sound hasn't changed that much. I use Marshall amps, but no, I tried different techniques. I like to use two microphones in front of the speaker and blend the two, the two mixed together. I learned that from Eddie Kramer. He used to use a 57 (Shure SM57) and a ribbon mic and blend them together, and now I've been using that technique forever."

Speaking with Sam Dunn, Kramer opined: "You can't really say Kiss are a heavy metal band. But they have elements of 'heaviness' to them, or metal to them. And that has been adapted, adopted, screwed with by other bands. But nevertheless, there is a classic example of a band who has religiously stuck with their fan base, and they want to make sure there's that core fan base that they satisfy every time when they put a record out. And yeah, sure, they've gone more commercial and all that. But it kicked them in the ass when they found that if they strayed too far, the fans would bite them back. But Kiss have a very unique position. In the history of rock, Kiss have done something really unusual.

"Just a very brief story about how I got to work with them. In 1972 it was Electric Lady Studios, and the studio manager at the time was managing a band called Wicked Lester. I'd seen Gene and Paul come into the studio and they'd done some tracks there, and I think they cut the album there. And it was a quote, unquote 'Beatles-type' album, kind of soft. Not very successful. In fact, that record went straight in the toilet, didn't come out.

"And this guy called me up and said, 'Hey, you know, Gene and Paul have this plan. They've got this idea of this rock band. Would you mind doing us a favor and just cut a demo for this band? It's called Kiss.' So, I said sure. I said if we're going to do this, let's do it the old-fashioned way. I'm going to cut it four-track, half-inch, which is how Hendrix and all this other stuff before in England did it. And we put them in Studio B, and I remember the band coming in. Gene or Paul I kind of knew because they'd been in the studio before. But in comes Ace

Graceland at three in the morning, demanding to meet with Elvis. In more productive news, *Alice Cooper Goes to Hell* is certified gold on this day.

On November 25, the Band perform their last show, at the Winterland Ballroom in San Francisco. There are a ton of guest appearances celebrating the send-off, deemed *The Last Waltz*, and Martin Scorsese is there to film the event. At the opposite end of the music business, EMI releases "Anarchy in the UK," the debut single by the Sex Pistols, who will dominate the headlines over the coming months.

To close out the month, on November 29, ZZ Top issue their fifth album, entitled *Tejas*. Billy, Dusty, and Frank have a great promotional machine of their own, with Bill Ham managing the band. Like Kiss with their fire-breathing show, ZZ Top attract a ton of publicity due to their *World Wide Texas Tour*, which features a bevy of Texas critters—snakes, buzzards, a Texas longhorn bull—live and

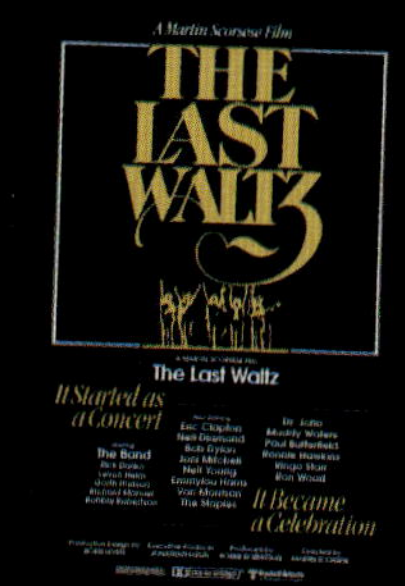

Frehley who was so skinny. I mean, if he turned sideways, you probably wouldn't see him. And, of course, the cat himself. So, we put this little demo together, a six-song tape, and that contained 'Black Diamond' and all the heavy hits, and that got them their record deal.

"I didn't produce their first record nor their second record, but this is a band that went out there and kicked ass for eighteen months and built up a core fan base that was undeniable. They sell one hundred thousand, maybe two hundred thousand records, small numbers relatively speaking. Okay, but not great. I remember one day I was sitting in my house. I'd just gotten married. It was maybe a year, year-and-a-half later, and I got this phone call from the West Coast. I lived in New York. It was the president of the record label, Neil Bogart, and he called me up and said, 'Hey, Eddie. I've got this band Kiss.' I said, 'Yeah, I know them; I did their demo.' He says, 'Yeah, I know. I want to make a live record with them. Would you be interested?' And I went, 'Neil, can I call you back in five minutes?'

"And I hung up and looked on my desk, and there was a tape sitting on my desk. I had to make up my mind really fast because I had to make a decision whether it was this tape from this one band or Kiss. And I called the gentleman's name on this tape box—it was Tom Scholz from Boston. I said, 'Tom, this tape is fabulous.' And it was—it was bloody marvelous. It was an incredible demo he sent me. I said, 'I can't do anything with this; I can't add anything *to* this—it's brilliant. Put it out.' I picked up the phone and said, 'Okay, Neil. I'm going to do it.' And the reason I did it is because, one, Kiss couldn't sing in tune, play in tune, play in time, or any of that stuff, because of their act. It was their act that was destroying everybody. Yeah, their songs were kind of cool and primitive and fun, but it was what they did onstage. And there was no way in hell . . . they're jumping around in boots that are yea high and makeup, spitting blood—how are you going to stay in tune and play in time? It's impossible.

"I mean, I say that now because that's how they were in the beginning. So that was the challenge for me. How do I get this band of crazy guys who are putting on a show with the music secondary? The show is the primary force. And that's why I called up Neil and said this is a challenge I can take on. That Kiss *Alive!* album basically saved Casablanca Records. And at the same time disco comes out, so you had the double-whammy of disco and Kiss. . . .

"I don't think that Kiss put their visuals on an even playing field with the music—I think it's their primary force. Certainly initially. And then as the band evolved and they became better players. . . . Certainly Ace. Ace was, for me, a great guitar player. Still is a much underrated guitar player. Crazy guy, wonderful guy. We did a great solo record with him. The rest of the guys were pissed off because it was the only one that sold and the rest of them tanked. But when you think of Kiss, that's Kabuki theater, it's Barnum & Bailey, it's the whole circus with the fireworks. People in the music industry, the critics, never really thought Kiss was serious. They knew they put on a great show, but they didn't think they were serious musicians. And as time went on, the playing got better, the shows got tighter, and the music became much more of a focus—or certainly an equal focus."

Kramer confirms that for *Rock and Roll Over*, on top of the above configurations, they also experimented with Peter on the stage, Gene and his bass under the stage, the vocals in the hallway, the guitars in various side rooms, all in pursuit of a live sound. They used a PA system, and they ran microphones all over the theater, which, incidentally, Gene says was partly owned by Frank Sinatra and later suffered a mysterious fire. Amps were isolated in various places, even under the stage, to keep them away from the drum mics, if and when the drums were not in the bathroom. Engineer Corky Stasiak was also impressed with Kramer's special "tube mics," which he had used with Jimi Hendrix and Led Zeppelin. Peter didn't want to use a click track, so Kramer kept time for him by banging on a wood box—he says he went through about twenty of them by the time they were done.

Once the basic tracks were sufficient, the operation moved over to the Record Plant, where overdubs were done, also quickly, from October 12 to 17. Final tweaks and mixing took place from November 18 to 24, while the band was across the country, resulting in an album that lives up to the brief in every way, namely back to the roots, get it done quickly, and get it into the shops. In fact, says Aucoin, part of the reason for getting albums out every six months was so the stores wouldn't return the previous album, just as it was about time to send back unsold copies. They'd be ready to pull the trigger, and Neil would tell them a new one was coming, so they decided to keep what they had left of the old one to keep a supply of the whole catalog, which would always get a boost from the new one coming in. Otherwise, says Aucoin, despite outward appearances, Casablanca would have gone bankrupt.

THE ALBUM COVER

The *Rock and Roll Over* album cover was done by Brooklyn-based graphic artist Michael Doret, who would eventually become a legendary figure in the world of logos, fonts, and typography in general. His most famed job besides *Rock and Roll Over* would be the redo of the New York Knicks logo in 1991, although at that time he'd done covers for *Time* magazine, which is what got Casablanca art director Dennis Woloch interested in him.

Doret was unfamiliar with Kiss but relied on his work with a Japanese art magazine for inspiration. Kiss were still superheroes at the end of the process but with more of a comic book flavor. The fact that you can turn the cover around and it will still read right-way-up was inspired by the words "roll over" in the title.

His initial sketch for the cover was done in pencil crayon, and once he showed it to the band, only minor changes were requested, most notably giving Paul more hair and a change of expression. As well, originally, Gene was grinning, comparatively. Ace and Peter are largely unchanged, save for Ace's mouth. The ring with the album title, rendered twice, was also rotated so that one of the two renderings read more neatly left to right. The printer worked directly from Doret's illustration,

clearly confused, onstage, much to the consternation of promotors everywhere. There were plans to release a live album celebrating the tour, but that didn't materialize, with ZZ Top missing out on a stratagem that had worked so well for Kiss in 1975 and then again in 1977.

As the blood flows, Gene transforms into the demon.

turning the color blocks solid using mylar overlays. This means that the only original that exists is the drawing done from colored pencils.

Doret also tweaked the Kiss logo a bit, returning some of the symmetry back to the two S's. The distinctive lightning strike augmentation was his idea as well. On the inner sleeve, that's turned into a four-way logo pattern that can also be turned around, always reading upright. Of course, the biggest triumph with respect to this right-side-up concept will soon be presented on another Casablanca album, 1977's *On Earth as It Is in Heaven*, where people see the classic, ingenious Angel logo for the first time.

Rock and Roll Over's back cover was largely a repeat of what was on the front, with the credits replacing the Kiss logos. Inside, there's the aforementioned four-way Kiss configuration on black background, an 8½" (21.5 cm) square sticker of the album cover, and an order form featuring merchandise on one side and Kiss Army questionnaire and ordering info on the other.

Woloch considers the *Rock and Roll Over* album cover art the band's most successful because being so flat and graphic, it was easy to reproduce on merchandise. Plus, it's been adapted for other projects over the years. Anthrax even parodied it for their live album, *Kings among Scotland*. Doret would also do the art for Kiss's 2009 album *Sonic Boom*, which clearly echoes his fine work on *Rock and Roll Over*.

Track by Track

"I Want You"

You've heard of false endings. Well, the first track on *Rock and Roll Over* begins with a false start. "I Want You" sounds like it's going to be the follow-up to "Beth," but then there's a churning electric guitar all on its lonesome before the song kerrangs into view. It's what the band did on "Black Diamond" and on "Rock Bottom," and kids ate that sort of thing up.

Paul says he wrote the song at a sound check in England on the band's first European tour, inspired to get creative by reflecting how he was now playing music on the same stages that all his British rock heroes played before him.

What emerges is the closest thing to a complicated and heavy *Destroyer* track that one's going to hear on *Rock and Roll Over*, followed closely by "Makin' Love" and nothing else. "I Want You" is also notable in that Paul plays the first guitar solo, with the second one handled by the band's usual lead player Ace. By the way, in his book, Paul expresses deeply his disappointment with Ace at this time, saying that he was a mess to the point where it became hard to get a solo out of him before he was passed out for the day.

"Take Me"

Paul admits that he was having a hard time writing new songs now that Ezrin wasn't around to help significantly in that department. So, he'd call Kiss Swiss knife Sean Delaney over to his apartment on Fifty-Second, and they'd come up with songs. As a result, there's three nice and neat Stanley/Delaney credits on the album, namely "Mr. Speed," "Makin' Love," and "Take Me"—he says these sessions also produced "All American Man," which is on *Alive II*.

Lyrically, Paul says "Take Me" is about the perks of being a rock star at the top of the world, especially the girls. Musically, fans are now seeing the downgrade from *Destroyer* to a sort of dumpy, clumpy simplicity, due in no small part to the bashed and trashy drumming. Also, here the beat is a sort of double-time thing, with the snare on one and three, whereas on the demo it's played straighter. Still, there are multiple riffs and even a twin lead—listen carefully, because there are some nice embellishments.

"Calling Dr. Love"

As previously mentioned, "Calling Dr. Love" evolved out of a Gene Simmons song called "Bad, Bad Lovin'," recorded in demo form in late 1975 in advance of the *Destroyer* sessions. Gene had recorded it with Katey Sagal, famed for portraying Peggy Bundy on *Married . . . with Children*, singing the backups. On the final version, it's Paul and Gene together doing the "female" response, singing falsetto. As for the title, Gene was inspired by a *Three Stooges* bit where "Calling Doctor Howard, Doctor Fine, Doctor Howard" comes over the intercom, after which Larry, Curley, and Moe, as doctors, race out of the office to attend to their doctorly duties.

"Calling Dr. Love" is another one that plays to the simplifying narrative. The chords are bare and obvious, and there's even cowbell, taking us back to the early 1970s. But there are nice sonic touches added to the display of the verse chords as the song moves along, and this one's got a groovy drumbeat. What's more, there's the fantastic snare drum sound Kramer and Stasiak dial in for Peter. Sensibly, perhaps, given that it was issued as the second single, it's the second most played song from the album in terms of Spotify numbers, behind the debut single, "Hard Luck Woman."

"Ladies Room"

Like the last song, "Ladies Room" evolved out of an old Gene demo, this one called "I Don't Want No Romance," which, in its demo arrangement, sounded like a cross between Bachman-Turner Overdrive and Creedence Clearwater Revival. The final actuality of the song has much more charm and, again, a gorgeous snare sound plus quality bass licks, rendered fat in the mix. Plus, that's Gene playing the boogie rock rhythm guitar. As Gene explains, it's about meeting a woman (or girl, as it likely was back then) and having to improvise with respect to location.

Once more the band was thinking about a good setup, a good pre-chorus, and they further draw attention to it by dropping out for a few simple cowbell whacks and a tom roll before giving us the chorus (third time around, Peter graduates to double-timing the roll). It's a warmly melodic song with a good groove, and Gene turns in an understated, albeit seductive, vocal. All told, it's shades of the Bay City Rollers' "Saturday Night," which can be said of the two previous tracks as well.

"Baby Driver"

As Paul frames it, Peter always thought he should have more song credits on the albums, but not being much of a writer, he'd bring in demos, often on cassette, from his old bands and propose them for reworking. "Baby Driver" originated from an old Lips song written about the band's bassist Michael Benvenga, who was more well off than Peter and guitarist Stan Penridge, and here he was, showing off his new Alfa Romeo Spider sports car.

The song indeed wound up getting a major renovation by the band, at which point Peter was all up in arms, picturing it slower and more soulful, to suit his love of soul music and his self-proclaimed soulful voice. In its final state, it's one of the heavier rockers on the album, and it's got the added feature of a trick beginning, where the "one" lands in an unexpected place once the song kicks in. It's one of two songs sung by Peter (although Gene sings on the demo), and he delivers a strong and somewhat bluesy vocal melody, set against the monotone backdrop of the supporting stabbing chords.

"Love 'Em and Leave 'Em"

As previously mentioned, "Love 'Em and Leave 'Em" has its roots in Gene's "Rock n' Rolls Royce" demo, which also influences "See You in Your Dreams." Again, which was somewhat the band's intention, the song sounds like it would fit on any of the first three albums, given its slapping, glam half-time rhythm (snare on one and three, identical to "Take Me"), and a riff that's a bit boogie or southern rocking. Peter gets in some tumbling tom fills, and indeed throughout, the beat is understated, with the song never allowed to lift off.

"Mr. Speed"

I remember as a kid thinking that next to "Hard Luck Woman," "Mr. Speed" was *Rock and Roll Over*'s worst track, with the band taking this simple, conservative, boogie rock thing too far, winding up tepid like Bachman-Turner Overdrive, Bob Seger, and Humble Pie.

But Paul seemed to like it, likely more so for the swaggering lyrics and also, one senses, as an example of some kind of platonic ideal of hooky songwriting, as practiced by Fleetwood Mac, the Eagles, Billy Joel, and Tom Petty—you know, for its universal connection with the maximum amount of people. Guitarist Bob Kulick and drummer Bill Lettang played on the original demo. Paul told Lettang to play like Charlie Watts, which gives you an indication of how he contextualized the song. Fair enough: Kids were thinking like metalheads, but Paul was playing 3D chess.

"See You in Your Dreams"

To these ears, this is the most charming of the suite of songs on this record that are stripped back but still acceptably heavy. It's got that recurring balance between boogie rock structure and modern power chording that is rife across the original trio of albums. But the power chording is a bit more power pop or pomp rock, like Cheap Trick or *Destroyer*'s "Do You Love Me." "See You in Your Dreams" is also the shortest song on the album, arguably accomplished by leaving out any form of pre-chorus. Still, it's got a spirited guitar solo, elaborate backing vocals, and a variant arrangement on the chorus that feels like a crowd sing-along moment.

"Hard Luck Woman"

"Hard Luck Woman" finds Paul experimenting with songwriting styles, pointedly trying to write like Rod Stewart, having been listening to "Maggie May" and "Mandolin Wind" and "You Wear It Well." As he puts it, and as is supported by the multitude of Kiss demos generated over the years, Paul is a good self-editor. He didn't think the song was right for Kiss and indeed tried to get it over to Rod Stewart himself to see if he wanted to record it. Funny thing is, if Rod's a good self-editor himself, he'd say, "I already have enough of these" or "It's too similar to this song that's going on the record." Amusingly, at the lyric end, Paul says he was inspired by "Brandy (You're a Fine Girl)," which was a smash hit in 1972 for Looking Glass (of note, bassist for the band, Pete Sweval, would wind up in Starz).

In any event, Kramer and Gene figured it would be a nice follow-up to "Beth," and given the Rod Stewart-ness of it, why not get Peter to sing it? Not that it was easy—Paul says it was like pulling teeth getting enough takes out of Peter, which, in the end, had to be spliced and diced to get what is heard on the album. To be fair to Peter, however, there was a heated difference in opinion, where Paul wanted Peter to sing it more like Rod, while Peter figured, just let me do it my way; given my voice, it's going to sound like Rod Stewart anyway.

As for the acoustic guitars, Kramer worked diligently to get a good sound, because it was obviously something that the band wasn't doing a lot of. As he has pointed out, both Paul and Ace play on it.

"Hard Luck Woman" became *Rock and Roll Over*'s lead single, doing much of the heavy lifting toward getting the record sold, especially to the small female demographic that the band could claim.

"Makin' Love"

Rock and Roll Over closes with its most squarely heavy metal track, therefore driving me and all my buddies crazy, despite the wolf-in-sheep's-clothing title of the song. Paul says it was inspired by "Whole Lotta Love," and you can hear that in the swooping vocal performance, albeit nowhere in the riff or wider musical structure. "Makin' Love" is just pure heavy metal, although there's the nice added touch in the pre-chorus with the acoustic guitars massaged in.

As the record closes out, note that there are no Ace credits, nor has Ace sung on a Kiss track yet. There are rumors that there was a song called "Queen for a Day" that Ace was supposed to sing, but he demurred. It won't be until *Love Gun* and the song "Shock Me" that fans will get to hear the Spaceman give it the ol' college try.

THE STATISTICS

As alluded to, the first single from *Rock and Roll Over* was "Hard Luck Woman," which got to #15 on the *Billboard* chart and that same position in Canada. "Calling Dr. Love" was the record's second and last single, achieving a #16 placement on *Billboard* and #2 in Canada. *Cash Box* had it at #10. The album itself reached #11 on the *Billboard* charts and #7 in Canada. It was certified gold upon release, meaning that advance orders exceeded five hundred thousand copies. Currently, it sits at platinum, a certification level it reached on January 5, 1977.

Larking about and posing backstage in Amsterdam.

If Kiss spent a lot of time in dressing rooms, well, it was because there was a lot of dressing to do.

Gene, Paul, and Peter are clearly on the same page. But what's with Ace's new look?

DECEMBER

Kiss wouldn't invade Japan until April 1977, but comic book heroes can dream.

DECEMBER '76 TOUR DATES

December 2	Mid-South Coliseum	Memphis, TN
December 3	Jackson Coliseum	Jackson, MS
December 4	Municipal Auditorium	New Orleans, LA
December 5	Municipal Auditorium	Mobile, AL
December 7	Von Braun Civic Center	Huntsville, AL
December 8	Macon Coliseum	Macon, GA
December 10	Jacksonville Coliseum	Jacksonville, FL
December 11	Sportatorium	Hollywood, FL
December 12	Civic Center Arena	Lakeland, FL
December 15	Memorial Auditorium	Buffalo, NY
December 16	Onondaga War Memorial	Syracuse, NY
December 18	New Haven Coliseum	New Haven, CT
December 19	Capital Centre	Largo, MD
December 21	The Spectrum	Philadelphia, PA
December 27	Cumberland County Memorial Arena	Fayetteville, NC
December 28	Roanoke Civic Center	Roanoke, VA
December 30	Augusta Civic Center	Augusta, ME

On December 1, "Beth" became a gold single in Canada, for sales of over five thousand copies. On January 5, 1977, it was certified gold in the United States as well. Three days later, "Beth" reached its *Billboard* chart peak at #7, near the tail end of a nineteen-week run on the grid.

The US tour in support of *Rock and Roll Over* continued, with the band playing Mid-South Coliseum in Memphis, Tennessee, on December 2; the Coliseum in Jackson, Mississippi, on December 3; the Municipal Auditorium in New Orleans, Louisiana, on December 4 (Blackfoot supports); and the Municipal Auditorium Mobile, Alabama, on December 5. Songs typically played from the new album included "Take Me," "Ladies Room," "Hard Luck Woman," "I Want You," and "Makin' Love." Dr. Hook was the main support early in the month, supporting their fifth album, *A Little Bit More*. Also on December 5, *Rock and Roll Over* was issued in Japan.

Continued on page 159

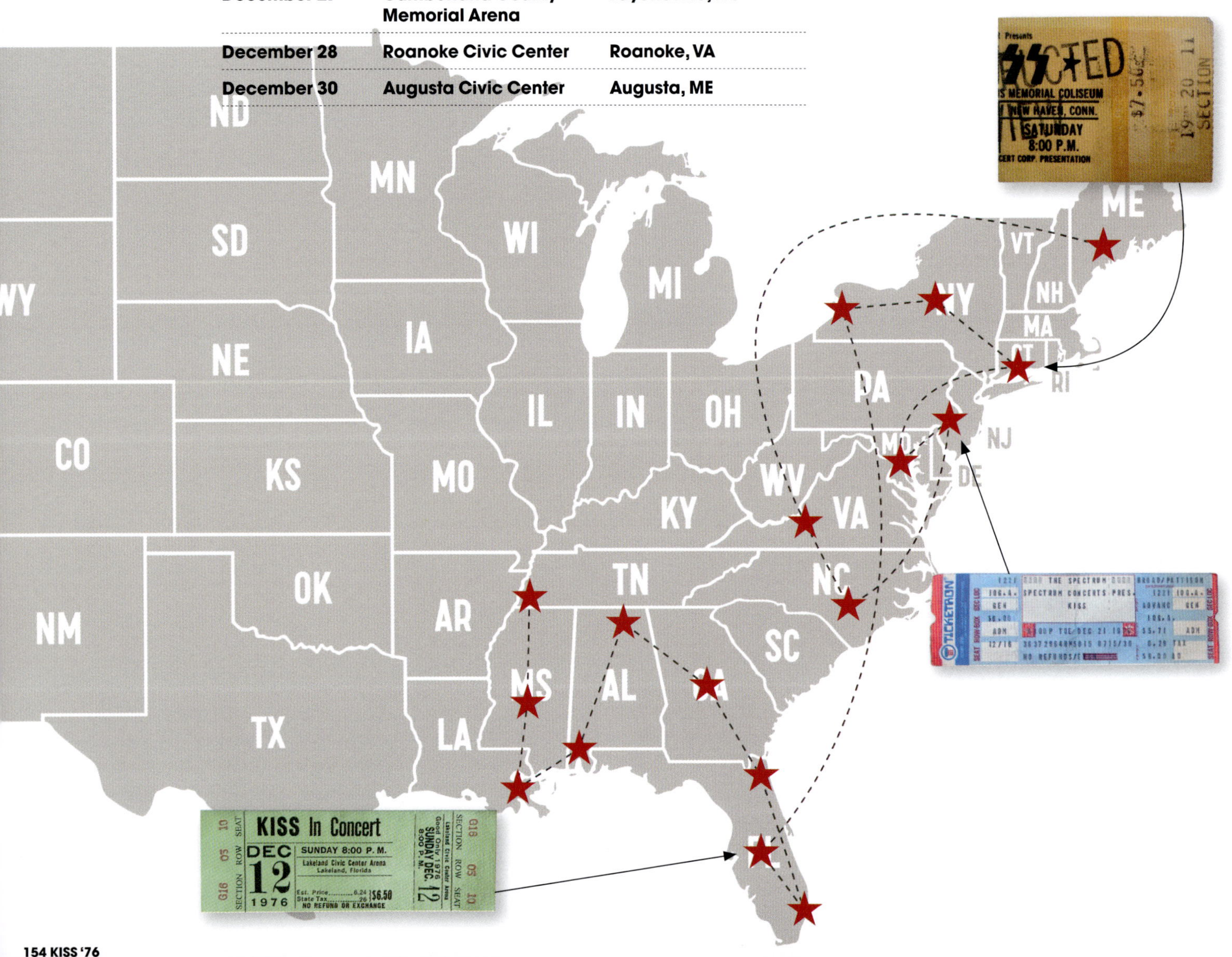

"What am I gonna do with this guy?!"

IN WORLD NEWS...

December begins with a new TV sitcom that becomes a hit with teenage boys called *C.P.O. Sharkey*. The US Navy–themed show stars Don Rickles, and soon the new catchphrase "I'm gonna keep an eye on you" begins making the rounds. Also in geopolitical news, the next day, Fidel Castro eliminates prime minster as

an official title and becomes president instead.

On December 16, the Louvre in Paris is invaded by masked robbers, and a number of artifacts are stolen, most notable including France's coronation sword. The next day, a remake of *King Kong*, starring Jessica Lange in her first major role, premieres in theaters. It reignites

Ace would end this momentous year in Lakeland, Florida, with the shock of his life.

interest in movie monsters among the Kiss fan demographic. There will be a further boost when Blue Öyster Cult's "Godzilla" becomes a hit the following year. Gene, as the God of Thunder, might have been a successful addition to that pantheon, but instead, in 1978, there was *Kiss Meets the Phantom of the Park*.

On December 20, Ned Washington, who wrote the lyrics to "When You Wish Upon a Star," dies at the age of seventy-five. Gene will cover the song on his 1978 solo album. Is that the closest Kiss ever got to doing a Christmas song? Five days later is Christ's birthday, and surprisingly Kiss never penned a Christmas carol, while their Casablanca doppelgängers Angel did, writing "Winter Song" in 1977. Angel also did a winter photo shoot that was similar to Kiss's famous session from this year. In the mid-1980s, on tour, Kiss will perform "White Christmas" live, with all four members singing it a cappella, barbershop-style, into one microphone at the front of the stage.

Not to be outdone by Ace, Gene figured he'd set his hair on fire.

On December 30, Bert Jones from the Baltimore Colts wins NFL MVP accolades, but the second- and third-place winners were more to a Kiss fans' liking. Jack Lambert was linebacker for the Pittsburgh Steelers, who were lauded for their "steel curtain" defense; indeed, the 1976 Steelers are often said to have had the greatest defense in NFL history. In third place was Kenny Stabler, quarterback for the Oakland Raiders—if you had long hair and wore a Raiders uniform, you sorta looked like Kiss.

The year ends on December 31, with the last CBS airing of the *Bicentennial Minute*. There were 912 episodes in total, beginning in mid-1974. Called upon to do the last one was outgoing President Gerald Ford, who also in his final month called upon Congress to declare Puerto Rico the fifty-first state of the union, a proposition that failed.

Peter winds down a dizzying but gratifying 1976.

IN MUSIC NEWS...

Contextually relevant records issued this month include *Flyin' High* by the hardest of southern rockers, Blackfoot, who would support Kiss just as the album was appearing in record stores. There's also the Babys' self-titled debut, with the new John Waite–led vehicle promoted heavily. Higher up the food chain is the Eagles' *Hotel California*, issued on December 8. It's currently the sixth-biggest-selling album of all time. The band's *Greatest Hits* compilation from earlier in the year is fifth. Closer to Kiss numbers are *A Day at the Races* from Queen and triple-live album *Wings over America*, both issued two days later. Paul McCartney's tour this year gets as much publicity as anything

On December 7, the band played the Von Braun Civic Center in Huntsville, Alabama, followed by a show at the Macon Coliseum in Macon, Georgia, on December 8, where Uriah Heep began a run of dates as support. Next was the Coliseum in Jacksonville, Florida, on December 10 and Sportatorium in Hollywood, Florida, on December 11. The issue of *Cash Box* dated December 11 included a full-page color ad promoting "Hard Luck Woman."

At the next show, Lakeland Civic Center Arena in Lakeland, Florida, Ace received a stiff shock when he touched an ungrounded handrail on his way down to the stage to launch into the band's set opener, "Detroit Rock City." After freezing in place, clutching the rail, he unfastened and fell several feet and was whisked back to his dressing room. After ten minutes of recovery, he returned to the stage and completed the show. Gene also set his hair on fire at this performance during "Firehouse." The incident with Ace caused the band to switch to wireless radio mics, inciting a wave of other bands to adopt the new technology over the ensuing months. The brush with death also inspired the song "Shock Me," which, as alluded to, also represented Ace's first lead vocal on a Kiss album.

The next stop on the tour was at the Memorial Auditorium in Buffalo, New York, on December 15, followed by the Onondaga War Memorial in Syracuse, New York, on December 16 and the Coliseum in New Haven, Connecticut, on December 18. Some of the posters advertising these shows featured art that sampled from both of the two recent album covers, utilizing the sort of buzzsaw blade design from *Rock and Roll Over* for the text but the *Destroyer* album cover for the depiction of the band.

Also on December 18, *Dressed to Kill* reentered the *Billboard* charts, peaking at #103 in January 1977. The issue of *Cash Box* dated this day reported that Casablanca's revenues for November were $4.4 million, making it the biggest month in the label's history, with March earlier in the year coming in second. There was also a curious separate piece where Neil Bogart was interviewed about the planned elimination of the 7" single, following sales declines. As everyone knows, singles will be around for years to come.

On December 20, 1976, Peter celebrated his thirty-first birthday, although most of the partying takes place the night before, after a show at the Capital Centre in Largo, Maryland. Next was the Spectrum in Philadelphia, Pennsylvania, on December 21, followed by a break for Christmas. Resuming right away, the band played the Cumberland County Memorial Arena in Fayetteville, North Carolina, on December 27; Roanoke Civic Center in Roanoke, Virginia, on December 28; and to close out a momentous year, the Civic Center in Augusta, Maine, on December 30.

As a bonus Christmas present, on December 25, *Rock and Roll Over* reached its *Billboard* peak position of #11, staying on the charts for forty-seven weeks. The album peaked at #7 in Canada. On December 29, manager Bill Aucoin celebrated his thirty-third birthday. The band got together and bought Aucoin a jukebox, which he installed in his fastidiously kept office. Aucoin spent his day at work looking over the proposed plotline for the upcoming Kiss comic book.

Kiss did, confirming the enduring appeal of the Beatles. In fact, George and Ringo were also regularly in the news in 1976, with only John Lennon absent, essentially out of his mind for a five-year period.

On December 1, the Sex Pistols appear on the *Today* show, produced by Thames Television. They are a last-minute replacement for Queen, which is somewhat symbolic. Eventually an incensed Bill Grundy encourages the band to swear, which Steve Jones accepts with gusto. Grundy will be fired, the show will be canceled, and the Sex Pistols will embark on one of their few and legendary chaotic tours.

On December 3, an inflatable pig used for a Pink Floyd cover shoot

Kiss '77: bathing in the glow of success.

works itself loose and escapes from its lines above Battersea Station in London. Meanwhile, in Kingston, Jamaica, there's an assassination attempt on Bob Marley. The following day, Deep Purple's Tommy Bolin dies—days earlier, he had been advertised as the support act for a Kiss show in Memphis on December 2. On December 28, another legend, bluesman Freddie King, passes at the age of forty-two.

Closing out 1976, representing a passing of the baton, the New York Dolls play Max's Kansas City on December 30. It is their final show before a reunion beginning in 2004. The following night, the Cars play their first show. Glam rock has given way to new wave, a transition

Kiss would effect or exercise as well, during the *Unmasked* period of the band in 1980, when the Cars were garnering all that excitement in the press that Kiss was getting four years earlier.

EPILOGUE

In Japan for a historic four-show stand, April 1, 2 (two performances), and 4, 1977.

Following are a few final comments about what happened with this special band after what they accomplished in 1976, which has got to stand as one of the busiest years in rock by anybody.

As alluded to earlier, as much as bands talk about how in the 1970s it was the norm to put out two records a year, it really wasn't that common. Plus, Kiss managed a triple compilation as well this year, along with two records in 1974 and a studio album and live album in 1975. They'd do one-and-a-half studio albums in 1977 and three sides of a live album as well, namely *Love Gun*, issued on June 30, and *Alive II*, which had the studio side, issued on October 14.

On top of that, they played live regularly; did photo shoots, interviews, and promotional appearances; and strategized with their manager Bill Aucoin on all manner of merchandising opportunity while also feeding their thriving fan club, the Kiss Army. They toured hard for nine months of 1977 as well, headlining Madison Square Garden for the first time in February and playing Japan for the first time in March. There were more gold and platinum albums, too, including certifications for the back catalog.

This space will not be used to talk about world events with respect to 1977 or, indeed, moving forward. That's for the anchor, or trunk, of the book, 1976—and that will suffice. As for Kiss's place against the rest of the music business, perhaps a few words are in order.

Kiss maintained their status throughout 1977 and into early 1978 as one of the biggest concert draws in North America, even if many other bands outstripped them with respect to album sales. They were also on par with pretty much anybody in terms of column inches in the press, aided and abetted by how good a picture they took. Aerosmith was flying high in 1977, as were Ted Nugent, Blue Öyster Cult, Boston, and Heart, who had a hit record in *Little Queen*. "We tried to sign Heart, right before they signed to Portrait," divulged Larry Harris, from Casablanca, "because we had somebody in our company who was good friends with Shelley Siegel, who owned Mushroom." Siegel died from a brain aneurysm on January 17, 1979, at the age of thirty-two.

The most remarkable success stories at this juncture were Fleetwood Mac, another act featuring two women, and soon, Foreigner. And let's not forget that Electric Light Orchestra continued to thrive in this intriguing melodic FM rock space. The Eagles offered no more records until 1979, but they remained a big deal. Led Zeppelin, the Rolling Stones, and the Who didn't have records either, but the heritage acts remained legendary, although only Zeppelin was properly active, conducting a landmark North American tour. Pink Floyd delivered *Animals*, and the Sex Pistols unleashed *Never Mind the Bollocks, Here's the Sex Pistols*.

How were Kiss's finances? Well, they were pretty dire even as *Destroyer* was emerging in March and April. By all accounts, the entire

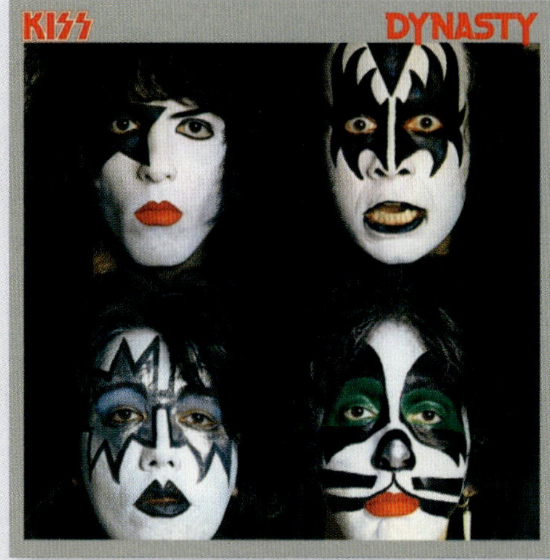

organization was saved by "Beth." But let's also credit the ambitions of the band, in particular Paul and Gene, along with Aucoin, who managed Kiss well, balancing risk with caution, leaning on a capable staff to make the operation almost military. And for all the drugs at the office and shortcuts taken and under-the-table payments for radio play, Casablanca operated more than acceptably—if it took on the personality of Kiss, it would be a little bit of Aucoin mixed with Ace. Indeed, the "party every day" mentality continued, fueled by record sales roughly equal between its four hit acts: Donna Summer, Parliament, Kiss, and newcomers Village People.

On September 18, 1978, each of the Kiss members issued solo albums, which followed a two-LP compilation called *Double Platinum*, issued on April 2 of that year. For all the accolades thrown at Ace's solo album these days, it's hard to remember any of them being particularly well received at the time. In 1979, the band issued *Dynasty*. A surprise disco hit with "I Was Made for Loving You" helped push the album platinum, but the band's reputation took a hit, which was soon felt at the concert box office. Explains Larry Harris: "When we sold half the company to Polygram in 1978, we used their money to grow the company even bigger. I mean, the Village People and Donna Summer and Parliament were huge. We had three movies. *Midnight Express* was an Academy Award winner; our first movie was *The Deep*. We just spent tons of money because when Polygram bought us, the deal was, they bought half the company and in five years they'd pay us ten times the profits after five years, to buy the rest of the company. So, Neil, being the big gambler, decided that he was going to roll the dice and spend their money to see how much money we could make.

"But the economy went into recession. A lot of people didn't have money to go see the shows. That generation was also growing up and having kids and getting jobs and having more responsibilities than they initially had. That changed everything. You had that new music coming that wasn't heavy metal and it wasn't straight rock 'n' roll; it was a mix. The Police were coming in, and there were a bunch of bands like that. You had people like Springsteen who were doing fine. The Stones were still touring and doing fine."

Unmasked (1980) and *Music from the Elder* (1981) perpetuated the slide for Kiss, and although *Creatures of the Night* didn't sell well initially, its reputation is now in a good place, as is the spate of records that found the band on firm but not hallowed ground throughout the 1980s. This is the thing with this band: They kept packing a lunch and going to work. Often losing money at a venue or across a whole tour, those records eked out their gold or platinum awards. Some think 1992's *Revenge* is the best record they ever did, and that helped them weather the grunge years (unlike their actual grunge album, *Carnival of Souls*). Bruce Kulick deserves a bunch of credit for this impressive run of records, with the band finding a steadiness in the lead guitar position after years of playing psychiatrist to Ace and Vinnie Vincent.

Next came a misstep with the parched *Psycho Circus* reunion album, but then again, the record was soon in the rearview mirror as the world celebrated Paul, Gene, Ace, and Peter appearing together again on live stages around the world.

Soon the band would settle in with Eric Singer on drums and Tommy Thayer on lead

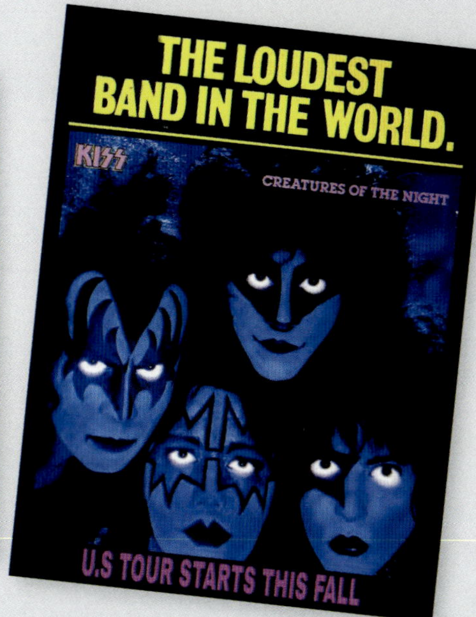

guitar, and two more fine albums, *Sonic Boom* and *Monster*, emerged, after which the band toured and toured before finally hanging up the boots with a momentous show at hometown Madison Square Garden on December 2, 2023.

But as insanely magical and constantly in the news the *End of the Road* world tour was, nothing can compare to the ignited excitement all of us teenage (mostly) boys had for Kiss in 1976. It's why a book like this had to exist, and it's indeed why a book celebrating the band's boldest year had to let the words range wider, taking in what was happening for us outside of our Kiss bubble, with other acts fans loved but also with other pop culture phenomena and world events.

Because even for dedicated soldiers in the Kiss Army—and perhaps in no small part because of what Kiss did for us throughout those twelve months—one might venture to say that everything to do with 1976 has turned into lucid and visceral memories, at least if you were at minimum entering your teenage years at that time. Hopefully, those memories are mostly fond ones. It is likely many of them are, comparatively, given what's happened to the world since, and as fans have lost their wide-eyed wonder and suffered any of the blows experienced in adulthood, despite, incredibly, Kiss being there for all of that, too.

In any event, that's the reason this book was constructed to be about 1976 as much as it is about Kiss. The hope is that it's been a journey that has reminded you—and enriched your understanding—of those times. And I hope, as it was for me, that it's been a swell look back at a magical moment in time—magical because of all the great records that came out, but magical mostly because of the series of searing explosions caused relentlessly, almost daily, by the hottest band in the land, Kiss.

Confusion reigned as Kiss cut their hair and said hello to the 1980s.

End of the Road—Madison Square Garden, December 1, 2023. They'd play the following night as well, capping fifty years of distinguished service, with no year more magical than 1976.

'76 TIMELINE

Here's some delightful afternoon perusing, themed specifically on Kiss-only milestones restricted to the anchor year of 1976. In the spirit of providing a hand-dandy survey of the key events in Kisstory—and for brevity—it is limited to the band's action-packed Bicentennial year.

January 13

Kiss present their new *Destroyer* costumes.

January 20

Paul celebrates his twenty-fourth birthday.

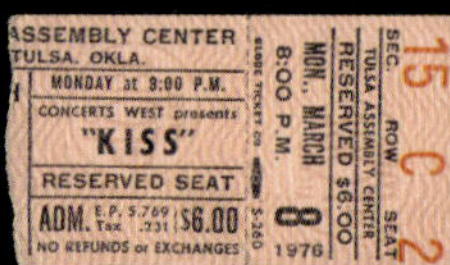

January 23 to March 28

Kiss conduct US tour dates in support of *Alive!*

April 11–28

Kiss conduct a North American East Coast tour leg.

April 22

Destroyer goes gold.

April 27

Ace celebrates his twenty-fifth birthday.

April 30

"Flaming Youth" is issued as a single.

May

Gene produces a demo for Van Halen, recording in Los Angeles and New York.

May 1

Ace gets married in Manhattan.

July 21

Kiss issue *The Originals*.

July 28

"Detroit Rock City" is issued as a single.

August 14

Kiss do an in-store at Peaches in Atlanta, Georgia.

August 19

"Beth" is issued as a single.

August 21

Gene conducts a photo shoot for *Creem* magazine with a hot rod car.

August 25

Gene celebrates his twenty-seventh birthday.

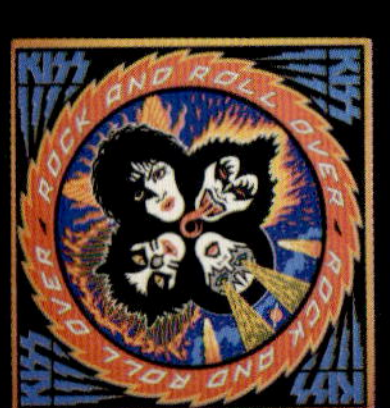

November 11

Kiss issue *Rock and Roll Over*.

November 11

Destroyer certifies platinum.

November 15–21

Kiss conduct dress rehearsals for their upcoming tour dates.

November 21

Kiss shoot promo videos for three *Rock and Roll Over* songs.

November 24

Peter sings "Beth" live for the first time in Savannah, Georgia.

December 1

"Beth" becomes a gold single in Canada.

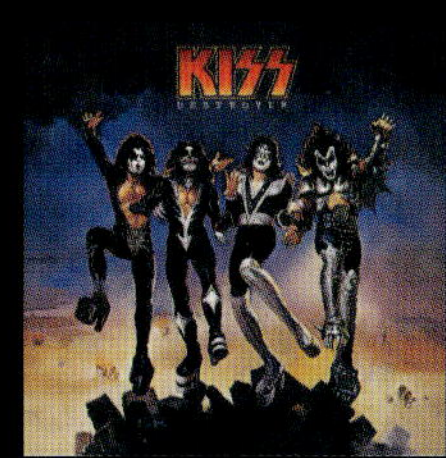

January 24

Kiss hold a formal press concert at the Detroit airport.

January 24

"Rock and Roll All Nite" (live) peaks at #12 on *Billboard*.

February 20

Kiss are added to the Hollywood Walk of Fame.

March 1

"Shout It Out Loud" is issued as a single.

March 15

Destroyer is released.

April 9

Kiss conduct a photo shoot with Barry Levine, Fin Costello, and Waring Abbott in Manhattan.

May 10

Kiss conduct a photo shoot at various locations around London.

May 13 to June 6

Kiss tour Europe in support of *Destroyer*.

May 15

Destroyer reaches its peak at #11 on the *Billboard* charts.

June 19

"Flaming Youth" reaches its *Billboard* peak at #74.

June 24

Barry Levine photographs Kiss atop the Empire State Building.

July 3 to September 12

Kiss conduct a full-scale US tour in support of *Destroyer*.

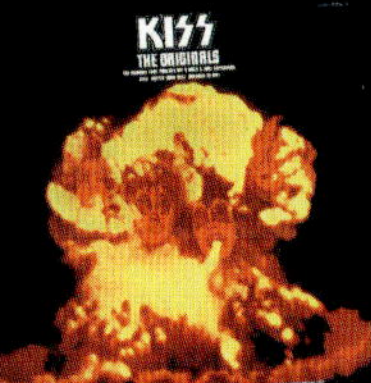

September to October

Kiss work on tracks slated for *Rock and Roll Over*.

September 25

The Originals reaches its *Billboard* chart peak at #36.

October 2

Destroyer reenters the *Billboard* charts.

October 29

Kiss appear on *The Paul Lynde Halloween Special*.

November 1

"Hard Luck Woman" is issued as a single.

November 7–12

Kiss rehearse at SIR Studios in New York.

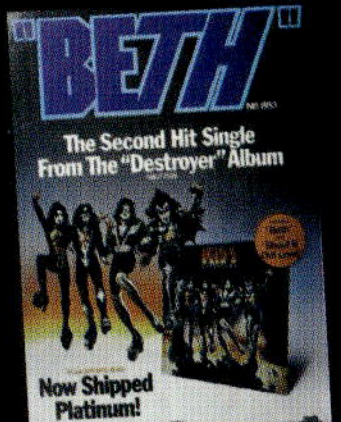

December 4

"Beth" reaches its *Billboard* chart peak at #7.

December 12

Ace gets electrocuted onstage in Lakeland, Florida.

December 18

Dressed to Kill reenters the *Billboard* charts.

December 20

Peter celebrates his thirty-first birthday.

December 25

Rock and Roll Over reaches its *Billboard* peak position of #11.

December 29

Kiss manager Bill Aucoin celebrates his thirty-third birthday.

KISS '76 DISCOGRAPHY

Here's a look at the three full-length albums Kiss stuck out in 1976, along with the singles and two promo EPs, all jumbled together in chronological order. This is United States only. Concerning a few points on format, there's an additional notes section for anything that seemed interesting and, er, notable. There are quote marks around songs for the singles entries only, just to keep things tidy. Side 1/Side 2 designations are noted because this was, of course, when there were vinyl records. The "Calling Dr. Love"/"Take Me" single, despite both being *Rock and Roll Over* songs, is not included because it was issued in 1977.

"Shout It Out Loud"

(Simmons/Stanley/Ezrin) 2:38/"Sweet Pain" (Simmons) 3:20.

Released March 1, 1976; Casablanca NB 854.

Destroyer

Released March 15, 1976; Casablanca NBLP 7025.

Recorded September 3–6, 1975, and January to February 1976 at Electric Lady and Record Plant, New York, NY.

Produced by Bob Ezrin.

Side 1: 1. Detroit Rock City (Stanley/Bob Ezrin) 5:30; 2. King of the Night Time World (Kim Fowley/Mark Anthony/Stanley/Ezrin) 3:15; 3. God of Thunder (Stanley) 4:20; 4. Great Expectations (Simmons/Ezrin) 4:20.

Side 2: 1. Flaming Youth (Frehley/Stanley/Simmons/Ezrin) 2:55; 2. Sweet Pain (Simmons) 3:20; 3. Shout It Out Loud (Simmons/Stanley/Ezrin) 2:50; 4. Beth (Criss/Stan Penridge/Ezrin) 2:45; 5. Do You Love Me (Fowley/Ezrin/Stanley) 3:33.

Notes: Additional guitar by Dick Wagner on "Flaming Youth," "Sweet Pain," and "Beth." Orchestration by H.A. MacMillan. Piano on "Beth" and assorted keyboards by Bob Ezrin. The orchestra on "Beth" is the New York Philharmonic.

"Flaming Youth"

(Frehley/Stanley/Simmons) 2:39/"God of Thunder" (Stanley) 4:20.

Released April 30, 1976; Casablanca NB 858.

Notes: This was Kiss's first US picture sleeve single. Bob Ezrin is missing from the A-side song credit.

"Hard Luck Woman"

(Stanley) 3:29/"Mr. Speed" (Stanley/Delaney) 3:19

Released April 30, 1976; Casablanca NB 873.

Special Kiss Tour Album

Released June 15, 1976; Casablanca KISS '76.

Side 1: 1. Beth (Criss/Stan Penridge/Ezrin) 2:45; 2. Do You Love Me (Fowley/Ezrin/Stanley) 3:33.

Side 2: 1. Flaming Youth (Frehley/Stanley/Simmons) 2:55; 2. Detroit Rock City (Stanley/Bob Ezrin) 5:30.

Notes: White label promo EP sent to radio stations in support of US *Destroyer* tour dates.

The Originals

Released July 21, 1976; Casablanca NBLP 7032.

Side 1: 1. Strutter (Stanley/Simmons) 3:10; 2. Nothin' to Lose (Simmons) 3:26; 3. Firehouse (Stanley) 3:18; 4. Cold Gin (Frehley) 4:21; 5. Let Me Know (Stanley) 2:58.

Side 2: 1. Kissin' Time (Kal Mann/Bernie Lowe) 3:52; 2. Deuce (Simmons) 3:05; 3. Love Theme from Kiss (Stanley/Simmons/Criss/Frehley) 2:24; 100,000 Years (Stanley/Simmons) 3:22; 5. Black Diamond (Stanley) 5:11.

Side 3: 1. Got to Choose (Stanley) 3:52; 2. Parasite (Frehley) 3:01; 3. Goin' Blind (Simmons/Stephen Coronel) 3:34; 4. Hotter Than Hell (Stanley) 3:30; 5. Let Me Go, Rock 'n Roll (Stanley/Simmons) 2:16.

Side 4: 1. All the Way (Simmons) 3:17; 2. Watchin' You (Simmons) 3:45; 3. Mainline (Stanley) 3:50; 4. Comin' Home (Stanley/Frehley) 2:37; 5. Strange Ways (Frehley) 3:17

Side 5: 1. Room Service (Stanley) 2:58; 2. Two Timer (Simmons) 2:59; 3. Ladies in Waiting (Simmons) 2:47; 4. Getaway (Frehley) 2:45; 5. Rock Bottom (Intro: Frehley/Stanley) 3:55.

Side 6: 1. C'mon and Love Me (Stanley) 2:54; 2. Anything for My Baby (Stanley) 2:30; 3. She (Simmons/Stephen Coronel) 4:05; 4. Love Her All I Can (Stanley) 2:43; 5. Rock and Roll All Nite (Stanley/Simmons) 2:45.

Notes: A repackage/compilation consisting of the first three studio albums, *Kiss, Hotter Than Hell,* and *Dressed to Kill.*

"Detroit Rock City"

(Stanley/Bob Ezrin) 2:57/"Beth" (Criss/Stan Penridge/Ezrin) 2:45

Released July 28, 1976; Casablanca NB 863.

Notes: The A-side is presented in greatly edited form. The A-side and B-side were switched the following month, issued August 19, with the catalog number remaining the same. Neither was a picture sleeve single in the United States.

Kiss Special Edition

Released November 1976; Casablanca NBLP 737

Side 1: 1. I Want You (Stanley) 3:02; Hard Luck Woman (Stanley) 3:32.

Side 2: 1. Take Me (Stanley/Sean Delaney) 2:53; Baby Driver (Criss/Stan Penridge) 3:39; Love 'Em and Leave 'Em (Simmons) 3:41.

Notes: A promo-only sampler EP sent to radio stations in support of *Rock and Roll Over.*

Rock and Roll Over

Released November 11, 1976; Casablanca NBLP 7037.

Recorded September to October 1976 at Star Theatre, Nanuet, NY.

Produced by Eddie Kramer.

Side 1: 1. I Want You (Stanley) 3:02; 2. Take Me (Stanley/Sean Delaney) 2:53; 3. Calling Dr. Love (Simmons) 3:41; 4. Ladies Room (Simmons) 3:25; 5. Baby Driver (Criss/Stan Penridge) 3:39.

Side 2: 1. Love 'Em and Leave 'Em (Simmons) 3:41; 2. Mr. Speed (Stanley/Delaney) 3:19; 3. See You in Your Dreams (Simmons) 2:31; 4. Hard Luck Woman (Stanley) 3:32; 5. Makin' Love (Stanley/Delaney) 3:12.

SOURCES

Billboard. "Casablanca Exposure Investment: Label Wagers Big Money to Avert Playlist Problem." March 20, 1976.

Cash Box. "Kiss Dominates *Cash Box* LP Chart; 4 LPs in Top 40." November 27, 1976.

Dayton Herald Journal. "Kiss live review." February 2, 1976.

Dunn, Sam. "Interview with Eddie Kramer." March 2010.

Freedland, Nat. "Outdoor Gigs a Kiss Kiss-off." *Billboard,* May 1, 1976.

Frehley, Ace, with Joe Layden and John Ostrosky. *No Regrets: A Rock 'n' Roll Memoir.* New York: VH1 Books, 2011.

Hit Parader. "*Alive!* review." Issue no. 141, April 1976.

McGee, David. "Kiss: A National Phenomenon." *Record World,* vol. 32, no. 1516, July 10, 1976.

McGee, David. "Bill Aucoin on Kiss, Rock Steady and the Future." *Record World,* vol. 33, no. 1520, August 14, 1976.

McGee, David. "Success—It's Just a Kiss Away, Kiss Away." *Rolling Stone,* issue no. 209, March 25, 1976.

McGee, David. "*The Runaways* record review." *Rolling Stone,* issue no. 218, July 29, 1976.

Milward, John. "*Destroyer* record review." *Rolling Stone,* issue no. 214, June 3, 1976.

Niester, Alan. "*Alive!* record review." *Rolling Stone,* issue no. 203, January 1, 1976.

Popoff, Martin. Interviews with Bill Aucoin, Bob Ezrin, Ace Frehley, Larry Harris, Barry Levine, Gene Simmons, Paul Stanley, and Richie Wise.

Record World. "Hits of the Week." March 20, 1976.

Record World. "Casablanca Reports Biggest Week Ever." March 27, 1976.

Record World. "*Rock and Roll Over* Review." November 20, 1976.

Robinson, Lisa. "Rock & Roll Hotline." *Hit Parader,* issue no. 139, February 1976.

Robinson, Lisa. "Rock & Roll Hotline." *Hit Parader,* issue no. 146, September 1976.

Robinson, Lisa. "Rock & Roll Hotline." *Hit Parader,* issue no. 148, November 1976.

Robinson, Lisa. "Rock & Roll Over with Paul Stanley." *Hit Parader,* issue no. 153, April 1977.

Robinson, Richard. "The *Hit Parader* Interview. Kiss by Kiss. Peter, Gene, Paul & Ace Talk About It." *Hit Parader,* issue no. 147, October 1976.

"Single Picks." *Record World,* vol. 33, no. 1520, August 14, 1976.

Sippel, John. "Casablanca Debuting Limited Edition Albums." *Billboard,* August 21, 1976.

IMAGE CREDITS

B = Bottom, C = Center, L = Left, M = Main, R = Right, T = Top

Alamy Stock Photos: Endpapers (Gijsbert Hanekroot), 2 (Gijsbert Hanekroot), 10 (© Globe Photos/ZUMAPRESS.com), 11CR (CBW), 16BL (Pictorial Press), 33 (Waring Abbott/© Globe Photos/ZUMAPRESS.com), 36TR (Historic Collection), 37M (Laurens Van Houten/Pictorial Press), 52 (Jeffrey Mayer/Rock Negatives/MediaPunch), 69BR (Tetra Images), 72–73M (Gijsbert Hanekroot), 79BL (Mirrorpix), 83M (Gijsbert Hanekroot), 89BR (Archive PL), 99BR (INTERFOTO), 100B (Historic Collection), 101BL (Everett Collection), 121BL (Album), 130 (Jeffrey Mayer/Rock Negatives/MediaPunch), 132 (© Globe Photos/ZUMAPRESS.com), 133 (Jeffrey Mayer/Rock Negatives/MediaPunch), 139BC (JT Vintage), 140M (Jeffrey Mayer/Rock Negatives/MediaPunch), 148 (Gijsbert Hanekroot), 156M (© Globe Photos/ZUMAPRESS.com), 157M (Waring Abbott/© Globe Photos/ZUMAPRESS.com), 160B (Gijsbert Hanekroot), 164 (Ralph Dominguez/MediaPunch).

Robert Alford: 18M, 19T, 19CL, 19CR, 57M, 97, 98C, 102, 103T, 105M, 115M, 117, 121T.

Creative Commons: 17BL (Andre Cros, city archives of Toulouse CC BY-SA 4.0), 69BL (Chris Hagerman, Creative Commons Attribution 2.0 Generic), 77B (Alex Goykhman, CC BY-SA 4.0),90BC (Archives New Zealand, CC Attribution 2.0 Generic), 90BR (Robert Taylor, CC Attribution 2.0 Generic), 101BR (Smithsonian, CC0 1.0 Universal Public Domain Dedication), 111B (Nationaal Archief, CC0 1.0 Universal Public Domain Dedication), 129B (Martin Lee, CC Attribution-Share Alike 2.0 Generic).

Richard Galbraith: 36M, 38M, 41M, 42M, 45, 46, 49, 58–61, 99, 100M, 101M, 112M, 113M, 114M.

Getty Images: 5M (*New York Daily News Archive*), 6–7 (Ginny Winn/Michael Ochs Archives), 9 (Steve Morley/Redferns), 11M (Fin Costello/Redferns), 13 (Fin Costello/Redferns), 15T (Fin Costello/Redferns), 16M (Fin Costello/Redferns), 17M (Fin Costello/Redferns), 21 (Fin Costello/Redferns), 23M (Fin Costello/Redferns), 24M (Fin Costello/Redferns), 25M (Fin Costello/Redferns), 26M (Michael Ochs Archives), 27M (Michael Ochs Archives), 27B (Bettmann), 28M (Armando Gallo/Michael Ochs Archives), 29M (Armando Gallo/Michael Ochs Archives), 30M (Armando Gallo/Michael Ochs Archives), 31M (Armando Gallo/Michael Ochs Archives), 35M (Michael Ochs Archives), 40M (Fin Costello/Redferns), 47 (Bobby Bank/Getty Images Entertainment), 50 (Fin Costello/Redferns), 51 (Mark Sullivan), 54 (Armando Gallo/Michael Ochs Archives), 56 (Fin Costello/Redferns), 62–63 (Fin Costello/Redferns), 65 (Fin Costello/Redferns), 68M (Fin Costello/Redferns), 69M (Fin Costello/Redferns), 70M (Michael Putland/Hulton Archive), 75 (Anwar Hussein Collection), 78B (Focus on Sport), 84–85M (Michael Putland/Hulton Archive), 91B (*New York Daily News Archive*), 92–93M (*New York Daily News Archive*), 94–95M (David Tan/Shinko Music), 104M (David Tan/Shinko Music), 109 (Roberta Bayley/Redferns), 111M (Fin Costello/Redferns), 116T (Tom Hill/WireImage), 119 (Michael Putland/Hulton Archive), 122M (Armando Gallo/Michael Ochs Archives), 123M (Tom Hill/WireImage), 124M (Tom Hill/WireImage), 125M (Tom Hill/WireImage), 127 (Fin Costello/Redferns), 128M (© Globe Photos/ZUMAPRESS.com), 129M (David Tan/Shinko Music), 135 (Fin Costello/Redferns), 138M (Fin Costello/Redferns), 149 (Fin Costello/Redferns), 150–151 (Fin Costello/Redferns), 153 (Michael Putland/Hulton Archive), 157B (Focus on Sport), 165 (Kevin Mazur).

Jeffrey Morgan: 67M.

PhotoFest: 87, 89T, 90, 91T, 137T, 139M,142–143M, 145, 155M, 158M, 160M, 161R.

Martin Popoff Collection: 7TC, 7BL, 18BL, 19BL, 19BR, 28B, 29B, 41BR, 42B, 42CL, 42BL, 42BR, 44B, 57BR, 70BL, 70BR, 72B, 76BR, 79BR, 82BL, 82BR, 84BL, 93B, 95B, 99CR, 103B, 104BR,106R, 114B, 116BL, 123BL,123BR, 130BL, 130BR, 132B, 133BL,140BL,140BR, 159CR,159BL, 159BR, 161L.

Public Domain: 37BL, 37BR, 105B, 113B, 121BR.

Frank White Photo Agency: 77M (Laurens Van Houten), 78M (Laurens Van Houten), 79M (Laurens Van Houten), 80–81 (Laurens Van Houten).

ABOUT THE AUTHOR

At approximately 7,900 (with over 7,000 appearing in his books), Martin has unofficially written more record reviews than anybody in the history of music writing across all genres. Additionally, Martin has penned approximately 135 books on hard rock, heavy metal, prog, punk, classic rock, and record collecting. He was editor-in-chief of the now-retired *Brave Words & Bloody Knuckles*, Canada's foremost metal publication for fourteen years, and has also contributed to *Revolver, Guitar World, Goldmine, Record Collector*, bravewords.com, lollipop.com, and hardradio.com, with many record label band bios and liner notes to his credit as well. Additionally, Martin has been a regular contractor to Banger Films, having worked for two years as a researcher on the award-winning documentary *Rush: Beyond the Lighted Stage*, on the writing and research team for the eleven-episode *Metal Evolution*, and on the ten-episode *Rock Icons*, both for VH1 Classic. Additionally, Martin is the writer of the original heavy metal genre chart used in *Metal: A Headbanger's Journey* and throughout the *Metal Evolution* episodes. Martin currently resides in Toronto and can be reached through martinp@inforamp.net or www.martinpopoff.com.

MARTIN POPOFF BIBLIOGRAPHY

2026: *Kiss '76*

2025: *Walking in the Shadow of the Blues: The Whitesnake Story, Taken by Force: Sixty Years of Scorpions, Midnight Mover: Accept '79–'96, Seven Decades of Deep Purple: An Unofficial History, A Million Vacations: The Max Webster Story, The Unholy Scriptures: The Complete Unofficial Chronicle of Ronnie James Dio's Solo Canon, A Dangerous Meeting: In the Shadows with Mercyful Fate, Guns N' Roses at 40, Hallowed by Their Name: The Unofficial Iron Maiden Bible, Blockbuster! The Sweet Story*

2024: *Judas Priest: Album by Album, Behind the Lines: Genesis on Record: 1978–1997, Entangled: Genesis on Record 1969–1976, Run with the Wolf: Rainbow on Record, Van Halen at 50, Honesty Is No Excuse: Thin Lizzy on Record, Pictures at Eleven: Robert Plant Album by Album, Perfect Water: The Rebel Imaginos*

2023: *Kiss at 50, The Electric Church: The Biography, Dominance and Submission: The Blue Öyster Cult Canon, The Who and Quadrophenia, Wild Mood Swings: Disintegrating the Cure Album by Album, AC/DC at 50*

2022: *Pink Floyd and The Dark Side of the Moon: 50 Years; Killing the Dragon: Dio in the '90s and 2000s; Feed My Frankenstein: Alice Cooper, the Solo Years; Easy Action: The Original Alice Cooper Band; Lively Arts: The Damned Deconstructed; Yes: A Visual Biography II: 1982–2022; Bowie @ 75; Dream Evil: Dio in the '80s; Judas Priest: A Visual Biography; UFO: A Visual Biography*

2021: *Hawkwind: A Visual Biography, Loud 'n' Proud: Fifty Years of Nazareth, Yes: A Visual Biography, Uriah Heep: A Visual Biography, Driven: Rush in the '90s and "In the End," Flaming Telepaths: Imaginos Expanded and Specified, Rebel Rouser: A Sweet User Manual*

2020: *The Fortune: On the Rocks with Angel, Van Halen: A Visual Biography, Limelight: Rush in the '80s, Thin Lizzy: A Visual Biography, Empire of the Clouds: Iron Maiden in the 2000s, Blue Öyster Cult: A Visual Biography, Anthem: Rush in the '70s, Denim and Leather: Saxon's First Ten Years, Black Funeral: Into the Coven with Mercyful Fate*

2019: *Satisfaction: 10 Albums That Changed My Life, Holy Smoke: Iron Maiden in the '90s, Sensitive to Light: The Rainbow Story, Where Eagles Dare: Iron Maiden in the '80s, Aces High: The Top 250 Heavy Metal Songs of the '80s, Judas Priest: Turbo 'til Now, Born Again! Black Sabbath in the Eighties and Nineties*

2018: *Riff Raff: The Top 250 Heavy Metal Songs of the '70s, Lettin' Go: UFO in the '80s and '90s, Queen: Album by Album, Unchained: A Van Halen User Manual, Iron Maiden: Album by Album, Sabotage! Black Sabbath in the Seventies, Welcome to My Nightmare: 50 Years of Alice Cooper, Judas Priest: Decade of Domination, Popoff Archive—6: American Power Metal, Popoff Archive—5: European Power Metal, The Clash: All the Albums, All the Songs*

2017: *Led Zeppelin: All the Albums, All the Songs; AC/DC: Album by Album; Lights Out: Surviving the '70s with UFO; Tornado of Souls: Thrash's Titanic Clash; Caught in a Mosh: The Golden Era of Thrash; Rush: Album by Album; Beer Drinkers and Hell Raisers: The Rise of Motörhead; Metal Collector: Gathered Tales from Headbangers; Hit the Lights: The Birth of Thrash; Popoff Archive—4: Classic Rock; Popoff Archive—3: Hair Metal*

2016: *Popoff Archive—2: Progressive Rock; Popoff Archive—1: Doom Metal; Rock the Nation: Montrose, Gamma and Ronnie Redefined; Punk Tees: The Punk Revolution in 125 T-Shirts; Metal Heart: Aiming High with Accept; Ramones at 40; Time and a Word: The Yes Story*

2015: *Kickstart My Heart: A Mötley Crüe Day-by-Day, This Means War: The Sunset Years of the NWOBHM, Wheels of Steel: The Explosive Early Years of the NWOBHM, Swords and Tequila: Riot's Classic First Decade, Who Invented Heavy Metal?, Sail Away: Whitesnake's Fantastic Voyage*

2014: *Live Magnetic Air: The Unlikely Saga of the Superlative Max Webster, Steal Away the Night: An Ozzy Osbourne Day-by-Day, The Big Book of Hair Metal, Sweating Bullets: The Deth and Rebirth of Megadeth, Smokin' Valves: A Headbanger's Guide to 900 NWOBHM Records*

2013: *The Art of Metal* (co-edit with Malcolm Dome), *2 Minutes to Midnight: An Iron Maiden Day-by-Day, Metallica: The Complete Illustrated History, Rush: The Illustrated History, Ye Olde Metal: 1979, Scorpions: Top of the Bill* (updated and reissued as *Wind of Change: The Scorpions Story in 2016*)

2012: *Epic Ted Nugent, Fade to Black: Hard Rock Cover Art of the Vinyl Age, It's Getting Dangerous: Thin Lizzy 81–12, We Will Be Strong: Thin Lizzy 76–81, Fighting My Way Back: Thin Lizzy 69–76, The Deep Purple Royal Family: Chain of Events '80–'11, The Deep Purple Royal Family: Chain of Events through '79* (reissued as *The Deep Purple Family Year by Year books*)

2011: *Black Sabbath FAQ, The Collector's Guide to Heavy Metal: Volume 4: The '00s* (co-authored with David Perri)

2010: *Goldmine Standard Catalog of American Records 1948–1991, Seventh Edition*

2009: *Goldmine Record Album Price Guide, Sixth Edition; Goldmine 45 RPM Price Guide, Seventh Edition; A Castle Full of Rascals: Deep Purple '83–'09; Worlds Away: Voivod and the Art of Michel Langevin; Ye Olde Metal: 1978*

2008: *Gettin' Tighter: Deep Purple '68–'76, All Access: The Art of the Backstage Pass, Ye Olde Metal: 1977, Ye Olde Metal: 1976*

2007: *Judas Priest: Heavy Metal Painkillers, Ye Olde Metal: 1973 to 1975, The Collector's Guide to Heavy Metal: Volume 3: The Nineties, Ye Olde Metal: 1968 to 1972*

2006: *Run for Cover: The Art of Derek Riggs, Black Sabbath: Doom Let Loose, Dio: Light Beyond the Black*

2005: *The Collector's Guide to Heavy Metal: Volume 2: The Eighties, Rainbow: English Castle Magic, UFO: Shoot Out the Lights, The New Wave of British Heavy Metal Singles*

2004: *Blue Öyster Cult: Secrets Revealed!* (updated and reissued in 2009 with the same title; updated and reissued as *Agents of Fortune: The Blue Öyster Cult Story in 2016*), *Contents Under Pressure: 30 Years of Rush at Home & Away, The Top 500 Heavy Metal Albums of All Time*

2003: *The Collector's Guide to Heavy Metal: Volume 1: The Seventies, The Top 500 Heavy Metal Songs of All Time*

2001: *Southern Rock Review*

2000: *Heavy Metal: 20th Century Rock and Roll, The Goldmine Price Guide to Heavy Metal Records*

1997: *The Collector's Guide to Heavy Metal*

1993: *Riff Kills Man! 25 Years of Recorded Hard Rock & Heavy Metal*

INDEX

Quarto.com

First Published in 2026 by Motorbooks, an imprint of The Quarto Group,
100 Cummings Center, Suite 265-D, Beverly, MA 01915, USA.
T (978) 282-9590 F (978) 283-2742

EEA Representation, WTS Tax d.o.o., Žanova ulica 3, 4000 Kranj, Slovenia.
www.wts-tax.si

30 29 28 27 26 1 2 3 4 5

ISBN: 978-0-7603-9884-5

Digital edition published in 2026
eISBN: 978-0-7603-9885-2

Library of Congress Cataloging-in-Publication Data

Names: Popoff, Martin, 1963- author
Title: Kiss '76 : twelve months that defined the hottest band in the land /
Martin Popoff.
Description: Beverly : Motorbooks, 2026. | Includes index. | Summary: "Kiss '76 is a photo-filled month-by-month look back at the year when Kiss became immortal rock legends"— Provided by publisher.
Identifiers: LCCN 2025029036 | ISBN 9780760398845 hardcover | ISBN 9780760398852 ebook
Subjects: LCSH: Kiss (Musical group)—Chronology | Rock music—United States—1971-1980—History and criticism | LCGFT: Chronologies
Classification: LCC ML421.K57 P6615 2026 | DDC 782.42166092/2—dc23/eng/20250715
LC record available at https://lccn.loc.gov/2025029036

Design: Burge Agency
Cover Image: Fin Costello/Redferns/Getty Images

Printed in Malaysia